W9-AZU-944

To

From

Date

Rain on Me

Rain on Me

Devotions of
Hope & Encouragement
for Difficult Times

by Holley Gerth

Holley Gerth
Numbers 6:24-26

Rain on Me

ISBN 978-1934770-49-8

Cover and interior design by Loveseat Creative. Interior layout by James Baker Design.

Published by Summerside Press, Inc., 11024 Quebec Circle, Bloomington, Minnesota 55438 | www.summersidepress.com

Summerside Press™ is an inspirational publisher offering fresh, irresistible books to uplift the heart and delight the mind.

Printed in China.

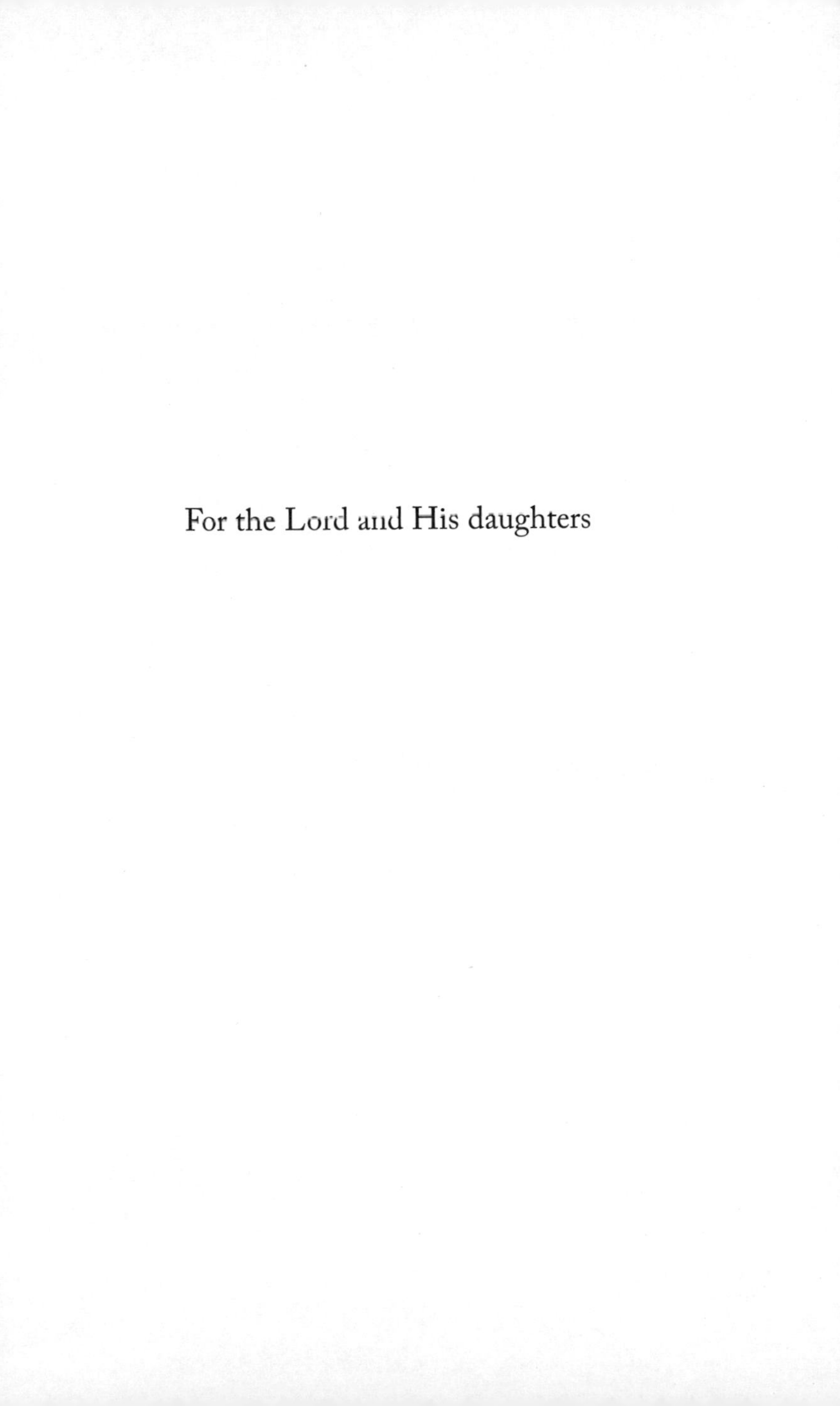

For the Lord and His daughters

Table of Contents

INTRODUCTION

Every Storm Begins with One Drop

Scientists recently discovered that raindrops hit the earth at speeds up to twenty miles an hour. Each one is like a miniature hammer pounding away dirt and scattering debris. Whether it's a small shower or a huge hurricane, raindrops make an impact.

Your first drop may have been a diagnosis given by a doctor with a grim face. Perhaps it was a note left on the kitchen table that said, "I'm sorry, but I don't love you anymore." It could have been a phone call late at night and someone on the other end telling you the unthinkable.

On the other hand, your first drop may have come so softly you didn't even recognize it. You tried to start a family and, after another negative pregnancy test, realized something might be wrong. You took a promising job and one day discovered that your computer screen might as well be a dead end sign. You began a relationship only to discover that your dream come true had started to feel a bit like a nightmare.

No matter how your first drop fell, it was probably followed by another...and another...and another. Now your heart is soaking wet and you're wondering if you'll ever feel warm and dry again.

The good news is, God knows even more about rain than those scientists. He knows the destruction it can bring. He also knows how to use it to bring beauty and hope to our lives. Take a quick look out your window. Every flower or tree you see owes its life to rain. Every bird singing, every frog hopping, every living thing draws its strength from storms.

I'm not saying God caused the storm in your life. We live in a broken world, and things are not as they should be. But I do believe that God is the Redeemer of the Rain. He longs to bring beauty out of brokenness, healing out of hurts, and new life out of losses.

I know this is true because I've experienced it personally. I'm not writing this book as someone who has stayed dry and watched others struggle outside my window. Several years ago God allowed a storm to brew in my life that I never expected when my husband and I began trying to start a family. Our infertility began as a drop, became a drizzle, and finally the heavens opened, and we found ourselves in an outright downpour when we lost our long-awaited baby to a miscarriage.

Over the past few years, there have been as many tears as there have been raindrops in my life. Through that journey, however, I've also seen what God can do with our greatest hurts and disappointments.

I've read many books in which the authors are looking back on the storms in their lives. This book is different because I'm still in the storm. I don't believe we have to wait for blue skies in order for God to use the rain. It can start right here, right now.

So wherever you are and whatever your storm may be, know that you are not alone. God is with you, and He is whispering messages about the rain to your heart that will change your world forever if you only dare to believe them.

I'm committed to walking through the rain with you, too. I'm praying for you as I write these words, and I'll still be praying for you as you read them.

May God redeem the rain in all of our lives.

—Holley Gerth

DAY ONE

It's Okay to Not Be Okay

I am convinced that neither death nor life, neither angels nor demons, neither the present nor the future, nor any powers, neither height nor depth, nor anything else in all creation, will be able to separate us from the love of God that is in Christ Jesus our Lord.

ROMANS 8:38-39

My grandmother has a cartoon on her refrigerator. It shows a cow on its back with all four legs in the air. The caption reads, "I'm fine, really, I'm fine." A lot of us handle the storms in our lives like that cow. We stand in the rain, soaking wet, with a smile on our faces, and say, "I'm dry, really, I'm dry."

I know what that's like because I did it for years. Somewhere along the way I was told, "Christians need to be happy all the time. If you're not happy, what will people think about Jesus?" If you want to breed a herd of perfectionists, just say that a few times from the pulpit.

For many years my life was mostly sunny. I could grin and bear it through the few showers that came along. But then came *The Storm*—the kind of storm that makes the weather channel flash maps covered with red and send warnings about taking shelter immediately.

It's one thing to stand outside in a nice little shower. It's another thing altogether to be that crazy news anchor hanging onto a light pole in the middle of a hurricane. I couldn't do it anymore. Like the rain that streamed down in my world, something opened in my heart, and hurt poured out from a place I had kept locked for years.

Then I waited. I listened for the rebukes. I watched for the disapproving stares. I stiffened my soul for the hard hand of God.

But instead of those things, I encountered the last thing I ever expected to find.

Love.

I felt it in the kindness of friends and family. I heard it in comforting words. I discovered it deep within my heart as God whispered, *I'm here with you.*

I also realized I wasn't the only one who was wet. People began to open up to me. Everyone I knew had some type of rain in their lives. We were one great, big, beautiful, soggy mess—and God loved us all.

So if you're still muttering under your breath, "I'm dry, really, I'm dry," then I invite you to admit that there's a storm in your life.

It's okay not to be okay.

When we embrace that grace, we're finally free to discover that love is waiting for us in the center of the storm.

Read

Romans 8:26-30

Reflect

What storm are you walking through right now?

What are you feeling as you walk through the rain?

How can you share those feelings with God and others?

Respond

Lord, my heart is in the midst of a storm right now. Please help me to be honest with myself and with You about all that I'm feeling. I especially want to tell You ______________________

Amen.

DAY TWO

Name That Hurricane

"Don't call me Naomi," she told them. "Call me Mara, because the Almighty has made my life very bitter. I went away full, but the Lord has brought me back empty. Why call me Naomi?"

RUTH 1:20-21

In 1953 the U.S. National Weather Service began using women's names for hurricanes. That lasted for a little over twenty years, until the women's liberation movement insisted that destructive storms be named after men too. The National Weather Service now uses six rotating lists of names that include both genders. If a storm is particularly deadly, the name is retired.

The purpose of naming a hurricane is to make it easier to track and understand. Now that you've admitted you're in a storm, I invite you to name it. Claim it as yours.

In the Bible names are powerful. When Naomi lost her husband and sons, she told people to call her Mara, which means "bitter" (Ruth 1:20). Naomi named her storm. She wanted everyone to know that raindrops of loss had fallen on her life until every last bit of hope had been washed away. Later in her story, we find that God brought hope to her again, but for this time she simply needed a way to address her pain.

What's the name of your storm? It could be loss, divorce, abuse, anger, addiction, infertility, brokenness, bankruptcy, chronic illness, death, depression, fear, guilt, or something else. Only you truly know the name your heart has spoken in the quiet moments and dark hours.

I invite you to write the name of your storm on a piece of paper that you can use as a bookmark as we go through these days together. You can use a note card, print something from your computer, or simply fold and tear a piece of paper. On one side write:

> the name of your storm
> when it began

On the other side, write a prayer about what you want God to do with that storm. For example, you might say something like:

> Lord, I'm naming the storm of ________________
>
> ____
>
> ____

before You today. I give it to You and pray You'll redeem the rain in my life. I specifically ask You to

during this time. Amen.

READ

Ruth 1

REFLECT

What did you name your storm? Why?

Briefly describe how your storm began and how it is affecting you now.

What is one thing God has shown you through this storm?

Respond

Write the prayer from your bookmark in this space as well.

DAY THREE

Where's God When It Rains?

He who dwells in the shelter of the Most High
will rest in the shadow of the Almighty.
PSALM 91:1

A few years ago, I read the book *Captivating: Unveiling the Mystery of a Woman's Soul*, by John and Stasi Eldridge.[1] In one part it challenges women to ask God how He's showing them His love. I was at the beginning of my storm during that time but still far enough into it to feel a bit abandoned, so I initially balked at the question. Finally, with a sigh, I silently asked, *Lord, how in the world are You showing me that You love me right now?*

In an instant the answer came. God spoke gently to my heart, saying, *I'm walking through the rain with you, and I'm giving you my umbrella.*

My mind flashed back to a day in college when an unexpected storm swept in while I was in class. I dreaded the long trek home. As I left the classroom, I couldn't believe what I saw. My boyfriend Mark (who is now my husband) stood waiting for me with a smile on his face and an umbrella in his hand. He had come to walk me through the rain. It's still one of the sweetest and most loving things anyone has ever done for me.

Of course the best part of the walk home that day was staying right beside Mark. Umbrellas aren't very big, and the closer you get, the drier you stay. It's the same way with God. I know what it's like to want to run away into the rain as fast as you can. I've done exactly that many times. However, the sweetest moments in my journey have come when I've chosen to stay under God's umbrella and let Him wrap His loving arms around me.

Being under God's umbrella still isn't like a walk in the park on a sunny day. There is an intimacy to it, though, that one day we may look back on with longing. We've all heard people say, "I'm glad that time in my life is over, but sometimes I miss how close I felt to God."

God is waiting outside the door of your heart to walk you through the rain. This may not be what you would have chosen, but it will be a journey you'll always remember.

Read

Psalm 91

Reflect

How is God showing you His love right now?

What do you think God is saying to your heart today?

Are you choosing to stay under God's umbrella or running into the storm? Why?

Respond

Lord, thank You for Your love. Sometimes it's hard to see in the midst of all this rain. I pray You will show me how You're taking care of me today. I especially need You to ______________________

____

____

____

Amen.

DAY FOUR

Foul-Weather Friends

Rejoice with those who rejoice; mourn with those who mourn.

ROMANS 12:15

A few years ago my dear friend Heather faced a particularly difficult time in her life. One day she wrote me an e-mail pouring out her heart, speaking of the sadness she felt. I remember reading that e-mail, staring at the screen, and desperately searching for the right words with which to respond. In my mind, I probably ran through all the Christian clichés I'd ever heard. I imagine that words of advice formed on my lips. Perhaps I even thought about a few similar experiences in my life and how those might be comforting.

In the end, however, nothing felt adequate. I didn't feel like a writer at that moment; I felt like a small, overwhelmed child searching for the right letters to form her very first sentence. So I did the only thing I knew to do. I bowed my head and asked God to fill in the blanks for me. While it doesn't often happen this way, the words below came to my heart in an instant.

> I wish I had a big yellow umbrella
> that would keep all the rain out of your life.
> I would hold it over your head,
> and the drops would splash, splash,
> and you would never even feel them.
> But I don't have a big yellow umbrella,
> so I'll walk through the rain with you.

Heather gratefully received those words and took me up on my offer. Over the next few years, we walked together through many storms in each of our lives. The message I sent to her eventually became a card that touched thousands of other lives.

Through that experience God showed me that we are not intended to go through our storms alone. We all need "foul-weather friends" who will venture out into the weather with us. Storms and sorrows both lose some of their strength when they are shared.

Read

Romans 12:9-21

Reflect

Who will walk through the rain with you?

What makes it hard for you to share your struggles with others?

Who needs you to share their storm right now?

Respond

Lord, You didn't create us to go through life alone, especially in the hard times. I pray for friends who will walk through the rain with me. I know many of them are hurting too, and today I want particularly to pray for ____________,

____

____

Amen.

DAY FIVE

Highs and Lows

Be merciful to me, O Lord, for I am in distress;
my eyes grow weak with sorrow,
my soul and my body with grief.
PSALM 31:9

In the weather world, a depression is a low-pressure system that may form severe storms. One such storm is the hurricane. When first seen on radar, a developing hurricane appears only as a few wispy clouds, but it can gather increasing power and density, until it wraps itself into a snail-shaped mass of white that draws more and more power and moisture into itself. Eventually it becomes a monster on the move that is capable of wrecking a city or destroying hundreds, even thousands, of lives in just a few terrible hours. Forecasters keep a close eye on depressions because they know how dangerous they can become.

Emotional depression can be like this too. There is a difference between feeling down occasionally and having depression. One blows in and dissipates after a few days. The other gathers strength and gradually consumes more and more of our lives.

It can be tempting to ignore the warning signs and let the depression build until it turns deadly. By then all we can do is watch our relationships, jobs, health, and even our very lives be washed away in the torrent.

That's exactly what happened to the town of Galveston, Texas, in 1900. At the time it was one of the wealthiest cities in America. It had weathered bad storms before, so it seemed there was nothing to worry about when clouds began gathering on the horizon this time. In addition, the lack of the forecasting technology we have today made the severity of the storm difficult to detect. While citizens paid little attention, a storm brewed that eventually claimed the lives of 7200 people and destroyed the city. It's still one of the greatest disasters in the history of our country.

As Christians we can sometimes act like the residents of Galveston. We tend to deny depression exists. After all, aren't we so blessed? In the meantime the clouds are thickening in our hearts and the winds are howling louder within our souls.

Many godly people in the Bible experienced depression. Take a moment to read David's laments in Psalm 102. He describes many of the major symptoms of depression, such as distress, lack of sleep, loss of appetite, and withdrawal.

Depression is more than just another passing thunderstorm, and if you're struggling with it, I would encourage you to seek help from a trusted professional, such as a Christian counselor. To learn more about the symptoms of depression and find resources, visit *www.ecounseling.com* and search for "depression." This site is operated by the American Association of Christian Counselors and presents biblical perspectives on life issues.

Just as we cannot stop a hurricane from happening, we may not be able to prevent our sadness, but as we partner with God and other believers, we can take action to limit its destructiveness. Perhaps, like David, we may even be able to harness its power and use it to bring about God's purposes in our lives.

Read

Psalm 31

Reflect

What have you been taught about how God sees depression?

Could you be struggling with depression right now? How do you know?

If you are experiencing depression, what steps can you take to get help?

Respond

Lord, thank You that You created all of our emotions, including the negative ones. Give me wisdom to know when I'm simply experiencing sadness and when it might be something deeper. One thing that's weighing on my heart today is

Amen.

DAY SIX

The Beauty of Brokenness

Then He said to Thomas, "Put your finger here; see my hands. Reach out your hand and put it into my side. Stop doubting and believe." Thomas said to Him, "My Lord and my God!"

JOHN 20:27-28

There's an old story about two pots. One was perfect in every way. The other had cracks and broken places. Each day a woman filled the pots with rainwater she had collected and then carried them down the path to her home. The first pot felt proud that she never spilled a single drop. The other felt ashamed because no matter how hard she tried, she lost a lot along the way.

One day the two pots overheard the woman talking with someone who lived nearby. The neighbor exclaimed, "The flowers along your path are so beautiful! What's your secret?" The woman answered, "One of my pots is broken, and the water that spills out helps the flowers grow every day."

That story reminds me of a song called "By His Wounds,"

a collaboration featuring Mac Powell from Third Day, Mark Hall from Casting Crowns, Steven Curtis Chapman, and Brian Littrell. Each one sings Isaiah 53:5:

> But he was pierced for our transgressions,
> he was crushed for our iniquities;
> the punishment that brought us peace was upon him,
> and by his wounds we are healed.

I first heard this song while driving home from work one day. During that time my pain seemed especially pointless. I also felt concern that nothing good would ever come of it. *Lord*, I silently prayed, *how can you even use me when I'm so broken?*

As I paused and considered that question, the song above came onto the radio. When the music ended, I began to develop a new perspective on my hurt. I realized that through Christ's wounds we are healed and, because He lives in us, our wounds can bring healing to others too.

We think that we have to take what's broken and make it perfect in order to be used by God and bless others. God thinks in a completely different way, however. He took what was perfect, His Son, and made Him broken in order to bring us healing.

If you're sitting there wondering if God can use you because your life is not as it should be and your heart is aching, know that your greatest hurt will probably be your greatest ministry. Like the disciple Thomas, who doubted until he touched the scars of Jesus, some people in your life need to see your broken places more than your victories.

We're all like the second pot in the story. God sees purpose in our brokenness even when we don't, and He can use it to bring forth beauty that blesses those around us.

Read

John 20:24-30

Reflect

What broken places do you have in your life right now?

How might God be able to use those to help others?

Describe a time when a hurt in your life enabled you later to bring comfort or healing to someone else. ________________

____

____

____

____

Respond

Lord, I'm so glad our brokenness can be used to bring forth something beautiful. I ask You to do that in my life, especially in the area of ____________________________________
Please use my hurts to bring healing to others. Amen.

DAY SEVEN

Honest to God

Then the Lord answered Job out of the storm.

JOB 38:1

Job is the celebrity of suffering. Most of us are very familiar with the biblical account of how God allowed Satan to take Job's children, possessions, and even health from him. After these tragedies Job sat for many days with his friends and poured out his emotions to God. His expressions included sorrow, rage, despair, frustration, and even a desire for his life to end.

Finally "The Lord answered Job out of the storm" (Job 38:1). He asks Job a series of questions like "Where were you when I laid the earth's foundation?" (v. 4). At the end Job says, "My ears had heard of you but now my eyes have seen you" (42:5). What Job needed most weren't answers to his questions but rather an assurance that God was real and He was still in control despite all that had happened.

This story from Job reminds me of one from the movie *Forrest Gump.*[2] In the Vietnam War, Lieutenant Dan loses both of his legs after Forrest saves him from certain death. Rather than being grateful, Lieutenant Dan experiences increasing bitterness and despair.

He eventually joins Forrest on his shrimp boat. One day a horrendous storm mercilessly batters their vessel. Rather than retreating to the shore, Lieutenant Dan climbs the mast and screams into the wind at God. He vents his rage and despair in a spiritual confrontation that is difficult to listen to because it's so visceral and raw. But the next time we see Lieutenant Dan, he is swimming peacefully in the sea with a smile on his face. Forrest narrates the scene by saying, "You know what I think? I think that day Lieutenant Dan found God."

Both Job and Lieutenant Dan have discovered a truth many of us never find: *Whatever it is, God can take it.* We tend to tiptoe around God as if He's a weak old man who shouldn't be upset. Or we see Him as a heavenly avenger just waiting to send yet another lightning bolt our way. But He is strong enough to handle anything we share with Him and loves us unconditionally.

If you have only been sharing with God what you think He wants to hear, then perhaps it's your turn to climb the mast, give full voice to your anguish, and allow God the opportunity to speak to you in the storm.

Read

Job 38:1-7; 42:1-6

Reflect

What is something you're afraid to express to God?

Why haven't you shared it with Him?

What do you think would happen if you did?

Respond

Lord, thank You for Your unconditional love. I confess that there have been things my heart feels that I have hidden from You, and I want to bring those out into the open. Today I want to share with You ______________________________

Please bring Your grace and healing to this part of my life. Amen.

DAY EIGHT

Off the Porch

Blessed is he
whose transgressions are forgiven,
whose sins are covered.
PSALM 32:1

My childhood pet was a small dog named Stacey. She had a gentle nature and generally stayed out of trouble. She had one odd habit, though. We had a large covered porch where she could stay while we were away. The porch provided shade and shelter from any storms, but if it rained, we invariably came home to find Stacey perched on a small hill in the center of our yard rather than on the porch. When we opened the door, she would race in, shivering and cold, and stare at us accusingly, as if to ask, "How could you let it rain on me?"

You may be reading this and thinking, "I'm Stacey. God provided shelter for me, and I deliberately made the choice to step out from under it. I chose the hill instead of the porch.

What does that mean now?"

The truth is, we're all Stacey at some times in our lives. The Bible makes it clear that we have all sinned and fallen short of God's glory, but some of our choices bring more painful consequences than others do. If this is the case with your storm, there are a few things you need to know.

First, there's a difference between sin and being human. Sin is a deliberate choice to disobey. Making a human mistake is not rebellion. If your storm is a result of sin, you need to repent, confess your sin, and receive God's grace. You also need to forgive yourself, which can be the hardest part of all. If your storm is not the result of sin, you need to accept that you're human and let yourself off the hook.

Second, if you have an opportunity to get out of the storm and back onto the porch, take it. My dog may have wandered into the rain, but she came zipping back in as soon as we opened the door. For example, if you've hurt your marriage by an emotional or physical affair, end it. If your temper is wreaking havoc on your relationships, get help.

If you've already repented but the storm is still raging, it does not mean you are being punished. God gave us free will, and that comes with consequences. When He allows the consequences to happen, He's not being mean or vindictive. It doesn't even mean that He's angry or disappointed with us. Instead it's a reflection of the fact that He values our freedom and ability to make choices. When Jesus said, "You reap what you sow," He wasn't making a threat; He was simply describing the truth.

Finally, you can ask God to "redeem the rain" in your life. Romans 8:28 says God works *all things* together for good in our lives. There is not an exception clause in this verse, one that exempts our mistakes and sins. It says *all* things in our lives. This doesn't mean we should make a habit of sitting on hills in the rain, but it does mean we can ask God to use those times for His purposes in amazing ways we never expected.

Read

Psalm 32:1-7

Reflect

In what area of your life have you "gotten off the porch" and allowed yourself to be in a storm?

What is God asking you to do about it?

What steps are you willing to take today?

Respond

Lord, I confess to You that I have [*name your sin*]

I am truly sorry and ready to change. Please forgive me and help me open my heart and my life to Your grace. And as I go forward in my life, I'm asking You to redeem the rain in my life and use it for Your purposes. I am committing to "get back on the porch" by [*name the step you will take*]

Help me keep from running back out into the rain again in the future. Amen.

DAY NINE

Surrendering Our Safety

I have told you these things, so that in me you may have peace. In this world you will have trouble. But take heart! I have overcome the world.

JOHN 16:33

We live in a world where safety is valued. We use antibacterial gel to ward away germs. We go through extensive checks at the airport. We always put railings on stairs.

While we need to take precautions, there can be trouble when we transfer this way of thinking to our spiritual life. When we start believing "safety first" must be a verse in the Bible, we're headed for trouble.

There's a scene in *The Lion, the Witch and the Wardrobe*, by C.S. Lewis, when one of the children asks Mr. Beaver if the lion, Aslan, who symbolizes Christ, is safe. Mr. Beaver laughs at this question and answers, "Who said anything about safe? Course he isn't safe. But he's good."[3]

There's a vast difference between safety and security. Being safe means being protected from all hurt or injury. Being secure means knowing that no matter what happens; we'll be okay in the end.

God never promises us *safety*. We're never told that our lives will be free from storms, hurt, tragedies, or disappointments. We often quote verses like Jeremiah 29:11, which says that God has good plans for our lives. While this is definitely true, we sometimes misinterpret this message as meaning that nothing difficult will ever come our way. I was pondering some of these scriptures during a difficult season of my life, and God gently whispered to my heart, *I had good plans for my Son too—but they still included a cross.*

This morning I was reminded of God's message to me. I was in a coffee shop, seated next to a group of women who were talking about "the law of attraction" and how, if you just believe, good things will come your way. They even quoted Bible verses and talked about asking God for everything from men to money.

While I absolutely believe that God does answer our prayers and bring blessings, there was something missing from the conversation I overheard. There was no talk of the times when God doesn't bring us what we want. I couldn't help but wonder how these women would react when a storm blew in and their safety disappeared.

When I learned to ice skate, I was a lot like those women. I decided I'd do whatever it took to never, ever fall. With that aim, I inched along the ice and clung to the walls. Then one day the unthinkable happened. With one loud *smack!* my illusion of safety disappeared. But lo and behold, I survived. That experience finally gave me the courage to get away from the wall, take some risks, and skate in a totally different way.

You may be in a similar place today. Throughout your whole life, you've been playing it safe. You use emotional "antibacterial gel," have extensive systems to make sure your heart is protected, and cling to the rails of life. Despite all that, here you are in the middle of what you tried so hard to avoid.

Now you have two choices: You can head back to your corner and continue living in the illusion that safety is a possibility; or you can take God's hand, let Him lead you onto the ice, and begin to trust that even if you fall, He'll be there to pick you up.

Read

John 16:20-33

Reflect

What are your top three fears right now?

What false beliefs about God make it difficult for you to trust Him?

Find a scripture that replaces one of those false beliefs with truth, and write it here.

Respond

Lord, thank You that my life is in Your hands. You are the one who offers me ultimate security no matter what happens. I've been struggling with the fear of ____________________

____

I release this fear to You and ask You to replace it with trust in You. Amen.

Further Thoughts

DAY TEN

Water-Walking

Peter got down out of the boat, walked on the water and came toward Jesus.

MATTHEW 14:29

One of my favorite books is John Ortberg's *If You Want to Walk on Water, You've Got to Get Out of the Boat*. It's built around the biblical story of Peter walking on the water. Imagine for a moment what it must have been like for Peter to step out onto the waves in pitch darkness, with a storm howling around him.

Ortberg says,

> The water is rough. The waves are high. The wind is strong. There's a storm out there. And if you get out of the boat—whatever your boat might happen to be—there's a good chance you might sink. But if you don't get out of the boat, there's a guaranteed certainty that you will

never walk on the water.[4]

When life gets difficult, we all have a tendency to hunker down and take fewer risks. We shift our focus to preventing further loss, guarding what we value, and maintaining the status quo. Then along comes Jesus, at the most inconvenient time, asking us to take a leap of faith we never expected—especially not right now. In those moments we have an opportunity to walk on water, but doing so requires stepping outside of our comfort zones. Ortberg writes, "Your boat is whatever represents safety and security to you apart from God Himself. Your boat is whatever you are tempted to put your trust in, especially when life gets a little stormy."[5]

In the biblical story, Peter decides to take the risk. We usually stop just after Peter begins to sink and Jesus reaches out His hand to save him. However, I'm fascinated by what happens *after* this. The next verse says, "When they climbed into the boat, the wind died down" (Matthew 14:32).

Have you considered what that verse is saying between the lines? Peter got to walk on the water with Jesus all the way back to the boat! And when they made it, the storm subsided.

Jesus may be asking you to step out of the boat in some area of your life today. You look around yourself and think, *Not now, Lord! Wait until things settle down!* We're not sure about walking on water in general, but if we are going to do it, we'd much rather have the lake as smooth as glass and not even a breeze blowing.

But if you dare to take that step of faith despite your fear, it may be the very thing that brings you closer to Jesus, lets you experience more with Him than you ever imagined, and perhaps even leads you to the moment when the storm finally subsides.

Read

Matthew 14:22-33

Reflect

Recall a time in your past when the Lord asked you to take a step of faith and you did so. What happened?

In what area of your life is the Lord asking you to take a step of faith today?

What is holding you back? ____________________

____

____

____

____

Respond

Lord, I thank You that You have more in store for me than I can even imagine. I sense that You are asking me to take a step of faith by ____________________

____

Please give me the courage to step out and come to You. Amen.

DAY ELEVEN

Soaring above the Storm

Those who hope in the Lord
will renew their strength.
They will soar on wings like eagles;
they will run and not grow weary,
they will walk and not be faint.
ISAIAH 40:31

Beth Jones-Schall, the founder and president of Spirit of Success, recently shared a little bit with me about why she chose to include an eagle as part of her company's logo. "Eagles are the only birds who use storms to lift them even higher. They wait for the winds to come and then soar." The theme verse for Beth's business is Isaiah 40:31: "Those who hope in the Lord will renew their strength. They will soar on wings like eagles." Beth needs plenty of strength since she travels an average of fifty weekends out of the year, speaking to business people on topics like leadership skills and strategies for business growth.

I met her at one national convention, where she spoke about being a "tekton" in whatever God calls us to do. The

Greek word *tekton* means "excellent" or "a master in your trade." She explained that each time Jesus is referred to as a carpenter in Scripture, the word *tekton* was used in the Greek.

For most of his life, Jesus was known not as Messiah but instead as an ordinary carpenter who handled the tasks He was given in an extraordinary way. Beth's point was that being a *tekton* draws people to us and makes them more willing to listen when we share about the source of our strength and excellence.

I believe that part of being a *tekton* means choosing to be like the eagle when the storms of life come our way. We can take the difficulties in life and use them as a force that takes us higher than ever before. That isn't an easy thing to do, but God promises that if we'll spread our wings and yield to the winds He's allowed to come into our lives, He will give us the strength to soar.

When that happens, it opens the door for us to touch the lives of others as well. We have bald eagles that nest close to the office where I work. On the rare occasion when someone spots an eagle soaring, we all gather to watch. It's an amazing experience to see a "*tekton* of the sky" in flight. When something difficult happens to us but we accept the strength God gives and soar onward, people begin to watch us more closely and want to hear our story.

As we discussed earlier, that doesn't mean we should

pretend we aren't hurting, slap a smile on our faces, and say we're okay when we're not. What it does mean is that we have an opportunity to let others see our hurt and how we're letting God use it to renew our strength and even begin to soar despite our difficulties. Where others see obstacles, *tektons* see opportunities.

Read

Isaiah 40:25-31

Reflect

When storms come into your life, do you tend to sink or soar? Why?

Describe a time when you let God use a difficulty to take you higher. What's one thing you did then that you could do again now?

Name a *tekton* in your life who has soared during a difficult time. What can you learn from his or her example and apply to your life? ______________________________

____

____

____

____

____

Respond

Lord, I thank You that even the difficulties in my life can become a force that makes me soar higher than ever before when I give them to You. Today I choose to be a *tekton* in the area of ______________________________
by pursuing excellence and being more than a conqueror no matter what happens. Amen.

DAY TWELVE

Hearts Created for Hope

We know that in all things God works for the good of those who love Him, who have been called according to His purpose.

ROMANS 8:28

Dr. Gary Oliver and his wife Carrie are two of my heroes. Carrie went home to be with Jesus in July of 2007 after a brave battle with pancreatic cancer. Gary carries on in his work as a psychologist, writer, and speaker. I've been privileged to know him as one of my professors and a member of my church.

Throughout her illness, Carrie kept an online journal, and Gary still posts family updates on it (www.carrieshealth.com). In one of her entries, Carrie shared the following thoughts about hope:

> We were created for hope. Our bones were bred for hope. Our lungs can't breathe, our hearts won't beat, and our spirits can't thrive without

> it. God placed us in a world over which we have little control. And as if to compensate for this helplessness, He placed within our souls the capacity to hope—to hope for better times, to dream of better places, to pray for better outcomes, to seek better ways through life. Hope is more than optimism. Optimism is what we generate. Hope is God-given, a powerful, spiritual and psychological means for transcending the circumstances.[6]

Carrie clung to hope until the last day she died. It didn't come from believing she would be healed. Instead Carrie's hope came from knowing that she would be in the hands of her loving heavenly Father no matter what happened. She continues to instill that hope in others through the lives she touched and the book she wrote while she was here.

Over a year after her death, Gary still chooses to focus on hope as well. In addition to losing his wife, Gary has personally battled cancer five times and endured the loss of his son. Yet he recently reflected, "In life we can have a fear focus or a faith focus. We can have a problem focus or a promise focus. What we choose to focus on makes all the difference in the world as to how we experience life." Where many would see only tragedy, Gary continues to uncover the goodness of God. He sees love, laughter, and the gift of life everywhere he looks. Although he's honest about the fact that some days are incredibly difficult, the hope his beloved Carrie shared in the words above is always with him as well.

God, in His infinite love, wants to help us find the potential for growth and new life hidden within each raindrop that falls in our lives. That kind of outrageous hope is the legacy of Carrie and Gary Oliver, and the kind of hope God offers your heart today.

Read

Romans 8:28-37

Reflect

What does the word *hope* mean to you?

What are some unexpected flowers God has grown in your life through this storm?

How can you share the hope you've been given with someone else today? ______

______

______

______

Respond

Lord, thank You that You are our hope and we can trust in You no matter what happens. I pray You will use the storm I am experiencing now [*name your storm*], ______

______

to grow new flowers in my life in ways I never expected and help me appreciate even more the ones I've already been given. I don't fully understand yet how that is possible, but I receive Your promise to work all things together for good in my life. Amen.

DAY THIRTEEN

Soul Searching

I have loved you with an everlasting love;
I have drawn you with loving-kindness.
JEREMIAH 31:3

You'd never guess that petite Jamie Zumwalt is the mother of five children, runs a church/coffee shop n the seediest part of her town, and came close to taking her ›wn life at a point in her journey when she felt overcome ›y despair. Nevertheless, all that and more is true of this piritual dynamo I consider a newfound sister in Christ and ın inspiration. Jamie is also the author of *Simple Obsession*, a ›ook about discovering the tender heart of God.

Jamie's passion for helping others discover an intimate 'riendship with God came out of her own pain. She grew up ıs a preacher's daughter. At age eight she saw a movie about nissions at her church and felt called to be a missionary.)uring her teen years, however, Jamie found herself caught in the storms of abusive relationships, eating disorders, and depression.

Jamie vividly remembers how, on the day she almost lost her life, her Dad came running through the door of her hospital room to embrace her. After pouring out many of the secrets she'd kept over the years, Jamey asked simply, "How do I get back to Jesus?"

A few days later, she slipped into the very last row of a church close to her college campus. The pastor stood up and said, "We're going to watch a movie about missions tonight." As the film began, Jamie saw that it was the very same one she had seen as a little girl.

She knew God was asking her to fully surrender her life to Him. She says, "I sat in that pew in the back of the church and argued with Him." Finally she sensed the Holy Spirit whispering to her, *Do you think you can do a better job with your life than I can?* Jamie knew the answer, and that night became a turning point for her.

Soon after that moment of surrender, Jamie met her husband, John. Together they've served as missionaries in Asia. They are also the founders of Heart of God Ministries. God has led them to minister to everyone from exotic dancers to drug addicts, as well as training other missionaries.

Even though Jamie surrendered her life to God, she still struggled through intimacy issues with Him for many years.

The more she came to know His heart, however, the more she learned He really would take care of hers. Jamie has these words for other women who have also been hurt in the past:

> God has a dream for your life that may be different than what you expected. It's on the other side of the line of surrender that you'll find it. You can trust Him with your heart. He is your father, friend, and bridegroom. You are God's simple obsession, and His heart is tender toward you. Because of that, He wants to be your simple obsession, too.[7]

As Jamie has discovered, sometimes the beginning of victory is simply surrender.

Read

Jeremiah 31:2-10

Reflect

What past hurts make it more difficult for you to trust God?

What area of your life are you holding back from Him because of that?

How would your life be different if you released that to Him?

Respond

Lord, I've been hurt in the past. This has led me to be afraid to fully open myself up to You. I want to trust You completely with all my heart, so I come to You now and release the hurts of

I ask You to bring healing and wholeness as I fully surrender to You. Amen.

DAY FOURTEEN

Heaven Is Waiting

He will wipe every tear from their eyes. There will be no more death or mourning or crying or pain, for the old order of things has passed away.
REVELATION 21:4

There's a truth that needs to be spoken on these pages that none of us want to hear. We all want our story to be like the time Jesus calmed the storm and instantly all was well. But we live in a broken world and deep inside we all know…

Sometimes the storms don't stop.

Sometimes the chronic illness isn't healed. Sometimes the infertility never ends. Sometimes the relationship doesn't get better. Sometimes it just keeps raining.

I recently spoke about this with a friend of mine. Her adorable daughter has a disability that will affect her throughout her life. It also brings daily heartache to my friend and her husband, even though they love their daughter very much and are thankful to have her in their lives.

When I asked what brings hope in the midst of this difficult situation, my friend said, "I think about heaven and how my daughter will have a new body. This life is not the end. One day we'll be in a place that is perfect."

Randy Alcorn, the author of *Heaven*, echoes this when he says, "Knowing our suffering will be relieved doesn't make it easy, but it does make it bearable. It allows for joy in the midst of suffering."[8] He also assures us, "God promises to make up for the heartbreaks on this earth."[9]

It's important for us to be able to look forward to heaven because as much as we may pray for the weather in our lives to change, some storms will stay until we step into eternity. That means sometimes prayers will go unanswered, diseases will not be cured, and justice will remain undone.

Like Noah, however, we have a rainbow waiting for us at the end of the flood. It's made of God's declaration that once we pass from this life to the next, we will never again watch our lives being washed away.

God has promised to wipe away every tear from our eyes, and on that day, He'll take away every stormy cloud from our skies as well.

> Hold out! There comes an end to sorrow;
> Hope from the dust shall conquering rise;
> The storm foretells a summer's morrow;

The Cross points on to Paradise;
The Father reigneth! Cease all doubt;
Hold on, my heart, hold on, hold out.

—Mrs. Charles E. Cowman,
Streams in the Desert[10]

Read

Revelation 21:1-7

Reflect

What do you think heaven will be like?

What are you most looking forward to in heaven?

What hurts are you looking forward to God bringing complete healing to in heaven? ______

______

______

______

______

Respond

Lord, thank You that this life is not the end, that it's only the beginning of all You have planned for me. One thing I'm really looking forward to in heaven is ______

______

Until that time, I pray You will give me hope and a deep sense of anticipation when I think about the ways You will redeem the hurt in my life forever. Amen.

DAY FIFTEEN

Questions without Answers

"For my thoughts are not your thoughts,
neither are your ways my ways,"
declares the Lord.
ISAIAH 55:8

With every drop of rain, a quiet question comes to our hearts. It's only one small word, and yet it holds our whole world within it.

Why?

In my journey I've asked it a thousand times. I've experienced four years of infertility, and I'm still counting. I also said good-bye to a baby I loved but never got to hold because of a miscarriage. I remember the silent moments in the middle of the night when I would wake up to stare at the ceiling and ask God, "Why?"

There is something within us that wants to know the reason. It seems as if understanding could somehow lessen the pain. I was part of a grief support group, and I remember the facilitator asking everyone in the room, "Do you want to know why?" Every hand was raised. Then she asked, "Would it make the hurt go away?" We all slowly shook our heads as we realized that the answers we sought wouldn't necessarily bring the healing we needed.

In *A Grief Observed*, C.S. Lewis writes about the loss of his wife. Throughout the book he wrestles with his faith. Toward the end he writes, "When I lay these questions before God, I get no answer. But a rather special sort of 'No answer.' It is not the locked door. It is more like a silent, certainly not uncompassionate, gaze. As though He shook His head not in refusal but waiving the question. Like, 'Peace, child; you don't understand.'"[11]

As much as we want to know, there are many things on this side of eternity that we will never understand. As a member of a book-reading club, I once read a book about the Holocaust. At one point our discussion turned to why God would allow such horrors. At the time I had recently lost my baby, and it felt as if a small holocaust had happened in my heart as well. I remember saying, "I don't know, but I feel as if God is asking me, 'Will you love Me for who you want Me to be or for who I am?'"

I don't know about you, but I want a God who doesn't allow suffering. I want a God who lets all our dreams come true, who erases death, who heals all my hurts, and who does it now. But that's not the God we serve. Somehow we have to release those expectations and decide that, despite it all, He is good, He loves us, and we love Him.

One of my heroes, Angie Smith, wrote in her blog, *Bring the Rain*, about the loss of her daughter Audrey Caroline and compared it to Moses' mother releasing her son in a basket onto the river:

> Sometimes I think it's harder to believe the way I do, because I believe with everything in me that He could have changed the story. This line of thinking inevitably brings me to the question, "Why didn't He?" Many people have written me with the same question, and I want to tell you that I have thought it through many times, and I have come up with a great theological explanation that I want to share with you.
>
> I have absolutely no idea.
>
> What I do know is this:
>
> The Lord walks beside me as He walked beside Moses, and He knows me by name. He loves me, and I love Him. I pushed my baby through the reeds and never saw her again. And yet here I am, worshipping the God who allowed it.[12]

At some point, we all come to the place where we're asked to open our hands, release our questions, and embrace the One whose ways we do not understand but whose heart we know. And the moment we can finally trade our "why" for a "Who," the rest of our journey changes.

Read

Isaiah 55:8-13

Reflect

What questions have you been asking God that He hasn't answered yet?

What are you afraid will happen if you stop asking why?

Describe a time in your life when you didn't understand the "why" but came to see God's hand in the midst of it all.

Respond

Lord, I have many questions without answers. I want to know why storms happen in my life. But even more than that, I want to know Your heart. So I release the following question

____

____

Even if it's never answered this side of eternity, I will still love and trust You. Amen.

Further Thoughts

DAY SIXTEEN

Your Loss Résumé

The Lord has anointed me
to...comfort all who mourn,
and provide for those who grieve...
a garment of praise
instead of a spirit of despair.
ISAIAH 61:1-3

Jan Stockdale and her husband Tom know about loss. As owners of a funeral home, they're familiar vith grief, shattered dreams, and the pain of good-byes said oo soon. Jan is also the directional leader for a women's ninistry and teaches a class called "Interrupted Expectations," n which she helps people deal with loss and prepare for it in he future.

One of the assignments she gives her class members is vriting a "loss résumé." She tells them to go back through heir lives and list each time they experienced an interrupted xpectation. The answers she receives include experiences ou would expect, like divorce, death, and unfulfilled dreams. ut there are others that surprise those making the lists, like moving multiple times, harsh words overheard, and unmet hopes from long ago.

Jan always reads her own loss résumé aloud to the class. There are hurts scattered throughout her life like landmines laid even before she was born. She tells of losses that came without her choosing and others she embraced by her own free will. Each one has made an impact on her life. A few still bring tears to her eyes and a quiver to her voice.

Then she does something no one expects. She begins to fill in the other column of the sheet. For each loss, she reveals how God has brought gain out of the loss. Slowly she weaves a story of how there is a divine balance at work. She assures us this doesn't mean that for everything bad that happens, we'll receive something good. It's far more complicated than a simple plus or minus. It's more about *transformation*. In God's economy, even what looks like loss can become gain.

The Bible is full of this paradox. Christ's death brought us life. The last will be first. When we give, we receive. It's a strange, mixed-up system that makes no sense to our human hearts. It is, however, a promise we can cling to on the days when our hearts need hope.

There's a flower called the rain lily that grows in Mexico and South America. The bulb will only bloom after it rains. The very storm that seems to threaten its existence is really the only thing that will call forth life from it. What looks like loss to the lily becomes a catalyst for strength and growth.

At the end of class, Jan reads her list of losses once again, his time without adding the gains. Then she asks one simple question: "If you read my loss résumé, would you hire me?" The class sits in silence, too embarrassed to answer. Finally someone laughs and says what they all secretly want to say, "No!" Jan miles in return, pauses for a moment, and then quietly says what every loss-laden heart needs to hear: "Jesus did."

Read

saiah 61

Reflect

Write your own loss résumé on the next page.

(For example, under "Loss" you might write "breast cancer," then under "Gain" you might put "new friendships with other women who have battled cancer too.")

Respond

Lord, thank You for transforming loss into gain in ways I don't even fully understand. I especially thank You for doing o through [*name a loss out of which unexpected gain came*]

There are still some very tender areas of loss in my life where 've not yet discovered the gains, so I pray You will continue o bring healing to my life and heart. Amen.

My Loss Résumé

Loss	Gain

DAY SEVENTEEN

The "Yes" You Never Expected

He stilled the storm to a whisper;
the waves of the sea were hushed.
PSALM 107:29

A few years ago, a coworker came rushing up to my desk with good news to share. She exclaimed, "A ;reeting card you wrote has been nominated for an award!" asked her what kind of card it was, and she replied, "Baby ongratulations."

After she walked away from my desk, I sat in stunned silence or a few moments as I considered the irony. An infertile woman night receive an award for a baby congratulations card!

As I looked back over the past few years, several other imilar instances came to mind. I unexpectedly got to help levelop a line of baby gifts. I published three books for hildren.

Slowly the Lord began to reveal something to my heart.

I sensed Him softly whispering, *I've said yes to every prayer that has been prayed for new life to come through you. It has just been in a different way than you expected.* As I absorbed those words, tears came to my eyes. I knew it was true.

I also knew that I had believed a lie. That lie went something like, "You did something wrong, and so God is saying no to your prayers." I thought if I could just be better, then somehow I could earn what I wanted.

Now, though, I suddenly realized God had been saying yes all along. In that moment God "stilled the storm to a whisper" in my life. Before then all I could hear was the rain pounding against my heart, and the steady beat sounded like *no, no, no, no.*

You've heard that sound, haven't you? Late at night, when all is quiet. In the middle of the day, when you're caught off guard by a painful longing or unwelcome memory. In the morning, when you wake up to another day when things are not as they should be.

Yet if we listen closer, there is another sound. It's the heartbeat of our heavenly Father, and it's always *yes, yes, yes, yes.* Even when we don't understand, *yes*. Even when it's different than what we expected, *yes*. Even when it seems as if nothing good is happening at all, *yes*.

Over the next few months, five people told me on separate occasions that they felt God was going to bring new ife through my words. I hadn't told any of them what God had revealed to my heart, and it was further confirmation of what I'd sensed to be true. Not having a child still hurt, but I also found renewed peace in knowing that God was at work.

Perhaps it's time for you to ask your heavenly Father to "still the storm to a whisper" in your life and help you hear His voice in a new way. You just may discover a *no* in your life is actually a *yes* you never expected.

Read

Psalm 107:28-43

Reflect

What seems like a *no* in your life right now?

In what ways could it actually be a *yes* you didn't expect?

Looking back on your life, describe a time when what looked like a *no* was really a *yes* in God's plan.

Respond

Lord, sometimes it's hard to tell when You are saying *yes* because what You're doing looks and feels so much like a *no* to me. I pray You'll help me to see how You may be answering in a way I didn't expect in the area of

Speak to me in a new way today. Amen.

DAY EIGHTEEN

The Choice Is Yours

Choose for yourselves this day whom you will serve.

JOSHUA 24:15

My dear friend Mandy often passes along stories about her kids. She recently shared how, as a parent, she really tries to give them choices. After listing several options to her two-year old daughter, Meg, the response was, “Mommy, stop choicing me!”

We’re all like spunky little Meg sometimes. God says, “You can stay with Me, or you can go out on your own. You can have blessings or consequences. You can stay dry or get wet.” Sometimes free will doesn’t seem like such a good deal, and our hearts say, “God, stop choicing me!”

You may be thinking, *But God didn’t give me a choice! I never wanted to be in this storm.* That brings up an important distinction. Sometimes we don’t choose our circumstances, but we can still choose our response to them.

Joshua told the Israelite people, "Choose for yourselves this day whom you will serve" (Joshua 24:15). He *didn't* say, "Choose how you will feel about this." Instead he challenged them to decide who will be master of their lives, regardless of their emotions or situation.

Your feelings and circumstances will try to be the boss in your life. They'll give you convincing evidence that you should be dominated by them.

God sets an example for us of how to make proactive choices. In *Boundaries: When to Say Yes, When to Say No to Take Control of Your Life,* Dr. Henry Cloud and Dr. John Townsend say, "God defines Himself as a distinct, separate being, and He is responsible for Himself. He defines and takes responsibility for His personality by telling us what He thinks, feels, plans, allows, will not allow, likes, and dislikes."[13]

Not everything in the world has turned out the way God wanted. He didn't desire for sin or suffering to be part of our existence. However, He doesn't allow those things to change His character. He continues to make choices based on who He is, whatever the circumstances. We are made in His image, and He wants us to respond the same way to everything that happens in our lives.

No matter what we decide, though, God's unconditional love will still be there. Mandy loved Meg from the first moment she discovered her daughter existed. Meg's choices will not change that love, although there are definitely options Mandy would prefer for her daughter's life! God relates in a similar way to us as His children. Because He values relationships over rules, our heavenly Father will never "stop choicing us."

Read

Joshua 24:15-25

Reflect

What do you think are the benefits and challenges of free will?

Who or what are you serving today?

What challenging choice has God been asking you to make?

RESPOND

Lord, thank You for the gift of free will. I pray that You will help me serve You rather than emotions or circumstances. I especially pray for Your help in making the choice to ________

Amen.

DAY NINETEEN

Go with God

At the Lord's command the Israelites set out, and at His command they encamped.

NUMBERS 9:18

When God led the Israelites through the desert for forty years, He gave them the earliest form of GPS. A cloud signifying His presence hovered over the tabernacle. When the cloud moved, they moved. When the cloud stayed, they stayed. "Whether the cloud stayed over the tabernacle for two days or a month or a year, the Israelites would remain in camp and not set out; but when it lifted, they would set out" (Numbers 9:22).

The Israelites chose to stay in God's presence. I'm sure it was frustrating sometimes. I would have been tempted to say, "Moses, we've been here for a month. We could have been there by now. Can't we just head out and God can catch up? After all, we know where He wants us to go."

The classic devotional *Streams in the Desert* says, "Still God often keeps us waiting. Face to face with threatening foes, in the midst of alarms, encircled by perils, beneath the impending rock. May we not go?... There is no answer. The cloud tarries, and we must remain."[14]

Perhaps you're in a season of waiting. You're thinking, *Seriously, God, isn't it about time we get out of this storm?* But there is a purpose in the waiting. For God it's about the process rather than the destination. It's about walking with Him rather than crossing the finish line.

Artist Julie Sawyer Phillips learned this firsthand as she waited to adopt a child. She says, "I longed for many years to be a mom and didn't know if God would ever grant that desire." Julie and her husband John put in an application to receive a child, but nothing happened.

During that time they also arranged to have dinner with the daughter and son-in-law of the couple who ran the orphanage where they planned to adopt. The group prayed together and asked God to bless the child He had for John and Julie. She says, "It was a special time, and I walked away wondering what God might do."

Four days later the phone rang and a voice on the other end said, "We have a baby boy for you!" When Julie considered the time difference, she realized her new son had been born the very same day those prayers were offered on her behalf. During the years that Julie had been waiting, God had been working out every detail. Julie says, "I don't think that means we're supposed to sit there and do nothing. We were a very active part of the process. But I do think it's important to go with God, even if His pace or plan are different than ours."[15]

In the end, it's not about the destination but who shares our journey. And God wants to be with us every step of the way.

Read

Numbers 9:15-23

Reflect

What is a situation where you're waiting or feel "stuck" right now?

What is God asking you to do while you wait?

Describe a time in your life when something was worth the wait. Why was it worth it?

Respond

Lord, waiting is hard. I'm ready to move on to what's next. I pray that You'll help me to focus more on the process than making progress. I especially ask You to give me patience as I wait for

Thank You for Your perfect timing. Amen.

DAY TWENTY

Singing in the Rain

And I'll praise you in this storm,
and I will lift my hands,
for You are who You are,
no matter where I am,
and every tear I've cried
You hold in your hand.
You never left my side,
and though my heart is torn,
I will praise You in this storm.[16]

The words above are part of the well-known song "Praise You in This Storm," sung by Mark Hall of Casting Crowns. In *Lifestories: Finding God's "Voice of Truth" through Everyday Life*, Hall shares the story behind the song. It was actually inspired by a little girl named Erin, who lost her life to cancer at the age of ten.

Erin loved Casting Crowns and even had the opportunity to perform a dance she helped create especially for them. Erin's mom, Laurie, kept the band informed about her daughter's condition throughout her struggle with cancer. Those updates, including one where Laurie literally stood on the Word of God and read from the Scriptures over her dying daughter, touched Mark Hall deeply, and "Praise You in This Storm" is the result.

Laurie says about her final time with her daughter, "It was not like how I expected her last minutes to be. I thought I'd be hysterical, but I wasn't. She was where she always wanted to be. She told me when she was six years old that she couldn't wait to get to heaven. She said she had felt an emptiness in her heart, but when she asked Jesus into her heart, she never felt it again because Jesus had filled her and would never leave her. For the ten years she was on this earth, God used her in a remarkable, powerful way."[17] Laurie describes having a tremendous peace that was like a shower from the Holy Spirit.

Throughout the years of fighting cancer, Laurie and Erin both praised God through the storm as the lyrics so eloquently describe. The first verse of the song says,

> I was sure by now, God,
> that You would have reached down
> and wiped our tears away,
> stepped in and saved the day.
> But once again, I say "amen"
> and it's still raining.[18]

It's one thing to look back on the storm and praise God; t's quite another to raise your hands to heaven when the ightning is flashing and the thunder is roaring. It's only hrough the amazing grace of God that we can do so. Rather han drowning out our voices, the praise we give God during lifficult times is the most audible of all to the world.

The songs the world hears from our hearts are also for our healing. God desires our praises, but He doesn't need hem. However, He knows that *we* do. In the deepest, darkest noments of our lives, we need to affirm what is true: We are oved, there is a greater plan, and God is still in control. The vords we lift to heavens also lift our hearts from despair.

Like Erin and Laurie, we're all called to sing in the rain. Vhen we do so, our Heavenly Father hears every word, the vorld takes notice, and our hearts are never the same.

Read

Psalm 42

Reflect

Vhat do you find to be the hardest part of "singing in the ain" to God? Why?

What are some ways you can praise God during this time?

Who has inspired you by the way they've brought glory to God through a storm in their lives?

Respond

Lord, I choose to glorify You today regardless of how I feel. I praise You for

May the words of my heart touch Yours and be used to make a difference in the lives of those around me. Amen.

DAY TWENTY-ONE

Holding onto Hope

Let us hold unswervingly to the hope we profess,
for He who promised is faithful.
HEBREWS 10:23

I wear two rings. The ring on my left hand represents the commitment I've made to my husband. he one on my right hand is a simple silver band with the vord *Hope* inscribed on it. After experiencing a difficult eason in my life, I bought the ring to be a daily reminder of ny commitment to God and myself to live in hope no matter vhat happens.

Before this time in my life, I thought hope was an motion. Now, though, I've realized it's so much more. I wrote bout that in a greeting card for which I created the message:

> Hope is more than a word—
> it's a state of being.

It's a firm belief that
even if you don't know how,
even if you don't know when,
God will come through
and better days are ahead.
Life brings rain…
Hope dances in the puddles
Until the sun comes out again.

Hope comes from perseverance and a stubborn belief tha God is faithful even when the evidence suggests the contrary. Another woman who has discovered this is Terrie Miller. She waited seventeen years and lost four pregnancies before God miraculously granted the desires of her heart through her adopted daughter Bethany.

Terrie told me,

> I think one of the most important parts of this journey is learning to trust God. I don't mean the flippant kind of trust. It's easy for people to say, "You just need to trust God." It's much harder when you're in the middle of all this pain. But He is trustworthy. Through it all, God has given us an amazing story. I wouldn't have chosen this road, but He has been with us. I can look back and truly say every step was worth it. [19]

There were many times for Terrie when hope seemed o be gone. That's why it's important to make a conscious ommitment to living in hope rather than relying on our motions. My ring is a visible reminder to me of that truth.

In the movie *Cast Away*, the character played by Tom Ianks is stranded on an island for many years. When he eturns, he discovers his fiancé is married to someone else. At ne point she says, basically, "Deep down I knew you were live, but everyone else kept telling me I had to let go."[20]

The world or our circumstances may tell us, "Hope is lead. God is gone. There's nothing you can do." On those lays we have to remember that we're committed to hope no natter what happens. Even when we can't see it. Even when ve don't feel it. Even when all evidence suggests the opposite.

Committing to hope doesn't mean believing that one day ve'll get what we want. True hope is believing in unchanging ruths: that God is good, He has a plan, and we are loved. Like strong marriage, that kind of hope can see us through a ifetime of "for better or for worse."

Read

Hebrews 10:19-24

Reflect

What do you think it means to commit to hope? ____________

What is threatening your hope the most right now? ____________

What will help you hold onto hope in the future? ____________

Respond

Lord, I thank You that You are the "God of hope" (Romans 15:13). Please renew my hope in the area of ____________

Help me to commit to living in hope for a lifetime, no matter what happens. Amen.

DAY TWENTY-TWO

Make Every Day Count

Teach us to number our days aright,
that we may gain a heart of wisdom.
PSALM 90:12

Eliot Mooney was given ninety-nine days on earth. His parents, Matt and Ginny, had a birthday party on each one. At the celebration service for their son's life, Matt said, "Not a pulpit. Not a slick presentation. Not a best-selling book. But a six-pound boy with Trisomy 18 (Edwards Syndrome). God found great pleasure in taking a lowly thing in the eyes of the world and showing truth." A video sharing Eliot's ninety-nine days has touched thousands of people around the world. One of Matt and Ginny's favorite verses is 2 Peter 3:8: "With the Lord a day is like a thousand years."

The Mooneys did what few of us are able to do: celebrate even in the midst of sorrow. Sometimes the rain in our lives blinds us to everything else. Yet even in those moments, there are still beauty, joy, and blessings to uncover. In her article "Don't Forget to Live," for *Today's Christian Woman*, Candy Arrington expresses regret about a difficult time in her life. "My greatest regret after traveling that long road is not living life fully during the waiting years. Often I was absorbed with medical procedures, my emotional pain, and quite frankly, anger with God."[21] Looking back, she now encourages others to embrace the good along with the bad during challenging seasons.

About a year ago, the Lord impressed this on my heart as well. I'd been through several losses and felt utterly discouraged. One day I prayed, *Lord, I feel like I'm in a deep, dark cave right now.* Of course I didn't hear an audible response, but He did impress on my heart, *You may be in a cave, but you have a choice: You can sit in the dark, or you can diamond-mine your difficulties.*

I decided then and there that I wasn't leaving that cave in my life empty-handed. I was going to take every blessing I could find with me. There were still many days when all I did was sit on the floor of the cave and grieve, but I also walked away from that time in my life with treasures I would never have found otherwise.

We'll all spend times in the caves of life. Yet inspiring people like Matt and Ginny Mooney remind us with their grace and courage that even in sorrow there is still celebration. This life is a bittersweet journey, where tears and blessings often flow from the same source. As Matt Mooney said, "How do you measure a life? By years? By esteem? By productivity? We propose that Eliot's life be measured by impact. Thus, truly his was a full life."

In the end, life isn't about counting our days. It's about making our days count.

Read

Psalm 90:12-17

Reflect

What stands out to you most from the story of Eliot Mooney?

How can you make today count?

What do you want people to remember about you at the end of your life? ______________________________

____

____

____

RESPOND

Lord, thank You that each day of my life belongs to You. I pray that You will help me make this day count by ______________

____

____

Whatever I go through, redeem it and use it for Your purposes. Amen.

DAY TWENTY-THREE

Building a Firm Foundation

The rain came down, the streams rose, and the winds blew and beat against that house; yet it did not fall, because it had its foundation on the rock.

MATTHEW 7:25

Hurricane Katrina roared through New Orleans in August of 2005, leaving destruction in its wake. For years the authorities had been warned that the levee system might fail if it had to cope with the effects of a major hurricane hitting the city. During those fateful days, all of those fears came to life as the world watched.

We all asked, "Why wasn't anything done sooner?" There are many answers to that question. Perhaps the two most obvious are: No one ever thought it would happen, and things looked fine on the surface. Katrina didn't *cause* the problems with the levees; it just revealed the weaknesses that were already there.

Storms in our lives do the same. We can get along

fairly well when things are fine. But suddenly the hurricane comes, and we're left wondering what happened. Gordon MacDonald describes this in his book *Ordering Your Private World*. Rather than a hurricane, he uses sinkholes to explain this scenario. He says, "If we think about it for very long, we may discover the existence of an inner space—our private world—about which we were formerly ignorant. I hope it will become apparent that, if neglected, this private world will not sustain the weight of events and stresses that press upon us."[22]

Whether we're talking about weaknesses in levees or sinkholes that suddenly appear, the lesson is the same. There is an outer part of our world to which it is easy to give attention and care, but there is also an inner world that is essential yet easy to overlook until a crisis comes along.

Long before Hurricane Katrina or Gordon McDonald helped show us this truth, Jesus shared it during His time on earth. Basically, he told those listening to Him, "If you put into practice what I teach you, your life will be like a house built on a rock. You'll have a firm foundation, and the storms of life won't destroy you. But if you don't, you're setting yourself up for pain and destruction." (See Matthew 7:24-27.)

After Hurricane Katrina came, the city of New Orleans did some serious reflection. Teams of people gathered and asked, "How can we make sure this never happens again?" It's wise for us to do the same after a storm comes into our lives.

We can ask ourselves, *What weaknesses did this storm reveal? Where is my foundation strong, and where do I need to make repairs?*

Having difficulties come into our lives is not a matter of if but when. That's why Jesus makes it clear we need to be prepared. Yet He also promises that if we build our lives on Him, we can survive and thrive whatever life's weather.

Read

Matthew 7:24-27

Reflect

Where is your foundation weak? ____________________

Where is it strong? ____________________

How can you prepare for storms in the future?

Respond

Lord, thank You for allowing this storm to reveal things in my life that need to be strengthened. I pray You will help me in the area of ________________

Please show me how to build a firm foundation on You that nothing can destroy. Amen.

DAY TWENTY-FOUR

Bitter or Better

Above all else, guard your heart,
for it is the wellspring of life.
PROVERBS 4:23

At age twenty-nine, my grandmother contracted polio and was told she would never walk again. As a young wife and mother of two little girls, she wondered what her future would be like. During her hospital stay, the pastor of their church came to visit. He made one simple statement that changed everything for her.

The pastor said, "Frances, this can make you bitter or better." She chose to let it make her better. Despite her disability, my grandmother lived a happy, fulfilling life until the age of seventy-six. People often asked the secret to the sparkle in her eyes. This gave her an opportunity to share about the God she loved so dearly in spite of her difficulties.

Bitterness threatens all of us when we face a challenge

in our lives. It can taint our views and poison our hearts. The Bible tells us to protect our hearts because they are the "wellspring" of our lives (Proverbs 4:23). That principle reminds me of the warnings about acid rain that seemed to be on the news every night a few years ago. Acid rain is polluted precipitation that can cause damage to plants and wildlife. Rather than leading to life and new growth, acid rain threatens everything it touches. Every report on it notes something interesting: Humans are the cause. We're the ones whose actions have made it occur, and we're the only ones who can stop it.

Bitterness in our lives is the same way. It pollutes "the wellspring of life" in our hearts. It makes it more difficult for God to redeem the rain in our lives and turn it into blessings. We let bitterness into our lives when we believe lies like "God doesn't care. There's no hope. No one cares about what's happening to me." We're also the only ones who can stop those lies and replace them with the truth.

If acid rain continues to worsen and is left untreated, it could destroy life as we know it. Bitterness can also take away far more than the loss that first let it into our lives. It's up to us to choose to be "better rather than bitter" through the difficulties we face.

This isn't an easy process, and at times everything within us will protest that choice. In the end, however, the bitterness will give way to a sweetness we never expected—a sweetness my grandmother tasted and left as her loving legacy.

Read

Proverbs 4:20-27

Reflect

Which best describes you—bitter, better, or both? Why?

What lies tempt you to let bitterness into your life?

How can you protect your heart?

Respond

Lord, I pray You will help me guard my heart from bitterness. It's hard for me not to become bitter when I think about

---

Please bring healing and protection to me, especially in that area. Amen.

DAY TWENTY-FIVE

Real Resilience

But as for me, I will always have hope;
I will praise You more and more....
Though You have made me see troubles, many and bitter,
You will restore my life again;
from the depths of the earth
You will again bring me up.
You will increase my honor
and comfort me once again.
PSALM 71:14, 20-21

In 1824 a new word was added to the dictionary: *resilience.* When applied to people, it means the bility to bounce back. After crossing an ocean, fighting a var, taming a frontier, and creating a new country, the early mericans had certainly earned the right to include that vord in their vocabulary.

When I think of resilience today, the first person who omes to mind is my 87-year-old Grandpa Hollie. At this ime last year, he had a triple bypass and a valve replacement. recently got back from a trip to Yellowstone with him. uring our trip, he was usually the last one back in the car ecause he was busy taking pictures of everything he could ind. That's resilience!

The Bible gives us examples of resilience as well. The verses above show a pattern in King David's life. He says, "You will restore my life again" and "You will increase my honor and comfort me once again." He's looking back over his life and remembering God's faithfulness. He's also looking forward and saying, "I will always have hope. I will praise You more and more." Seeing God's faithfulness in the past, praising Him today despite our circumstances, and choosing hope in the future no matter what happens is a recipe for resilience.

In *Resilience: Rebounding When Life's Upsets Knock You Down*, counselor H. Norman Wright says, "There are three possible outcomes of a crisis: a change for the better, a change for the worse, or a return to the previous level of functioning. The word *crisis* is rich with meaning. The Chinese term for crisis (*weiji*) is made up of two symbols: one is for danger and the other for opportunity."[23]

Life is difficult. We will all have times when things don't turn out the way we expect, when loss takes us by surprise, when challenges threaten to overwhelm us. In those moment we will always grieve because that is how God enables us to process our losses. Yet even through tears, we can also embrace hope and choose to grow in understanding and strength—to live out true *resilience*.

READ

ʾsalm 71:14-24

REFLECT

-Iow would you define *resilience*?

n what ways has a difficulty you are facing now made you tronger for the future?

Vhat steps can you take to ensure you "finish well" in life, no natter what happens?

RESPOND

Lord, thank You for the strength You have given me so far. I pray You'll continue helping me run the race of life. I especially ask for resilience in ______________________

____

May I persevere and finish well, no matter what happens. Amen.

DAY TWENTY-SIX

Last on the List

Suffering produces perseverance;
perseverance, character;
and character, hope.
ROMANS 5:3-4

When I first read the verse above, I wondered if my Bible had a typo. Wasn't hope supposed to be at the beginning of the list? That's certainly where I wanted it to be. I didn't like the idea of going through suffering, perseverance, and character to get to hope.

My thoughts reflect our culture today. We view hope as an emotion rather than an outcome of choices we make. We also think hope should be automatic. Then when we don't find it right away, we despair. But this passage makes it clear that hope is a *process*.

The first step in that process is suffering. Loss is a part of life. We'll all endure hardship and heartache on this side of heaven. When we suffer, we have two choices: press on or give up. Jim Rohn once said, "We all must suffer from one of two pains: the pain of discipline or the pain of regret." [24]

If we choose discipline and perseverance, then this pattern gradually becomes part of who we are—our character. Character doesn't change based on circumstances or who is watching at the moment. As Dwight L. Moody said, "Character is what you are in the dark."

Character also becomes a light in the dark because it eventually results in hope. This kind of hope is not a vague feeling or wish. Instead it's a deep knowledge that you and God can get through anything together. In *Holding onto Hope: A Pathway through Suffering to the Heart of God,* Nancy Guthrie writes about how deep losses led her husband to experience God in a new way. She says, "Now that he has experienced his greatest fear, and experienced God's supreme faithfulness to us through his difficulty, he no longer fears tragedy in our lives. We know God more fully because we've experienced Him more fully through our sorrow." [25]

That's the heart of hope: choosing to walk with God through the valleys of life and finding that He will never leave you—and that you will never leave Him either.

We all wonder how our faith will fare when challenges come our way. If you're reading this page, then you're probably choosing perseverance and character. You're facing what you never wanted, and your faith is surviving, perhaps even thriving. Even if you have doubts, fears, and many difficult moments, you're pressing on and moving forward. So take heart, dear sister, hope is on the way.

Read

Romans 5:1-5

Reflect

Does it surprise you that hope is at the end of this list? Why or why not?

Where do you think you are in this process (suffering, perseverance, character, or hope)?

What might God be asking you to do that could lead to more hope?

Respond

Lord, I pray You will meet me in the midst of my suffering today and help me to persevere. May this difficulty transform who I am, the very essence of my character. I especially pray for help to continue ____

____

Thank You for the hope You give me. Amen.

DAY TWENTY-SEVEN

Runaway Love

Praise be to the God and Father of our Lord Jesus Christ,
the Father of compassion and the God of all comfort,
who comforts us in all our troubles.
2 CORINTHIANS 1:3-4

The world mourned with beloved Christian musician Steven Curtis Chapman and his family when their five-year-old daughter was accidentally struck and killed by a vehicle driven by one of their sons. Only a few months after that tragic day, the Chapman family shared their story of hope in the midst of heartache on *Larry King Live, Good Morning America,* and *Focus on the Family* with Dr. James Dobson.

Each time I heard the story, one moving moment stood out to me. The Chapman's son Will Franklin was the one who hit little Maria Sue, and he was inconsolable. Once his parents came to the scene, he simply ran away. He said he didn't know where he was going, only that he was so overcome with emotion that he wanted to run and never stop. His older brother Caleb chased after and tackled him. Caleb told his brother over and over, "You can't go. You can't go."

At the same time, Steven was pulling out of the driveway to follow the ambulance to the hospital. Although he doesn't recall his exact words, those present later told him he rolled down the car window and loudly shouted a remarkable statement: "Will Franklin, your father loves you!"

Later Will Franklin said that those words, along with the love and support of his family, made all the difference. The whole family is still grieving and doesn't understand why this tragedy happened, but there are two things they have never questioned: their love for each other and the faith that holds them together.

At some point, we're all like Will Franklin. Brokenness enters our lives. Out of fear, hurt, and shame, we want to start running and never stop. But like Caleb, our older brother Jesus chases us down and tackles us. He holds us close to his heart and whispers over and over, "You can't go. You can't go." Then our heavenly Father shouts to us as loudly as He can, "Daughter of Mine, your Father loves you!"

Wherever you are today, whatever you are questioning, there are some things that will always be true. The God who has seen the brokenness still calls you His own and still loves you. He doesn't want you to run away but rather to run into

His arms, to find the healing your heart so desperately needs.

While speaking through his tears about the death of his sister, Caleb Chapman once told an audience, "God didn't heal Maria Sue in the way we would have liked. But I think He's going to heal Will Franklin in a way we'll all like a lot."

May the God of redemption who is giving the Chapman family hope even in heartache do the same in all of our lives.

Read

2 Corinthians 1:3-7

Reflect

Are you running toward or away from God today? Why?

If God were to "roll down the car window" and shout a message of love to you today, what would it be?

Who has been Jesus to you—someone like Caleb Chapman—who brings you back to the place where you belong? ______

Respond

Lord, thank You that even when I run away, You pursue my heart and never let me go. Please show me Your love today. One thing You are speaking to me in the midst of my hurt is ______

Amen.

DAY TWENTY-EIGHT

I Second That Loss!

A righteous man may have many troubles,
but the Lord delivers him from them all.
PSALM 34:19

When loss comes to our lives, we usually describe it in simple terms:

"I lost my mother."
"I no longer have a job."
"My marriage is ending."
"The cancer is back."

But loss is like an onion, and beneath the primary loss, there are many others we often don't recognize. During a grief support group session, I listened as each person shared. One woman said, "I lost my best friend, business manager, lover, companion, gardener, and husband." She was wise enough to see that while the term *husband* did describe her loss generally, he had actually played several roles in her life. Now she was experiencing several losses, not one, and each one was a source of grief.

In *Recovering from Losses in Life*, H. Norman Wright calls these "secondary losses." He says, "These can be actual, visible losses or subtle changes involving our relationships with others, status, environment, living style, hopes, dreams, wishes, and fantasies."[26] He encourages people not only to recognize the primary loss and grieve for it, but also to name and grieve for the secondary losses as well.

The disciples experienced this when Jesus died. Their primary loss was that of a face-to-face, day-to-day relationship with their Messiah. However, they also lost a friend, companion, and teacher. Their dreams of Jesus rising to political power ended. Their expectations of sharing many more years in ministry with Him were never met. Jesus was resurrected, but their relationship with Him still changed forever.

Jesus knew this would be difficult for the disciples. In one of their last conversations, He said to them, "Do not let your hearts be troubled. Trust in God; trust also in me" (John 14:1). Even though His death was God's plan, it still involved complex grief for those who loved Him.

In the same way, the losses in our lives can be far deeper than we grasp. I recently spoke with a woman who asked, "Why am I not over this yet?" When I listed off several econdary losses, she said, "Oh, then it makes sense that I'm till grieving!" She was being overly hard on herself because he hadn't recognized the scope of her loss.

To help you discover secondary losses, I would encourage ou to draw a circle in the middle of a piece of paper. Then lraw lines out from the inner circle that look like spokes on a icycle wheel. On each one, write a secondary loss that stems rom the original one. Then take a few moments to bring ach secondary loss to God.

This exercise may seem unnecessary, but if we grieve in n incomplete way, then it can come back to us in the future. Wright says, "When we don't grieve properly, unresolved eactions and feelings lead to a higher level of discomfort, and hese unresolved issues continue to prevent us from living life o the fullest."[27] But when the secondary losses you identified re wrapped in God's healing, they can become part of the wheel that moves you forward in hope.

Read

Psalm 34

Reflect

What secondary losses did you discover through the "wheel" exercise?

Which one surprised you most? Why?

What steps can you take to address and mourn those losses?

Respond

Lord, thank You that You know every hair on my head and every loss in my life. I pray that You will help me to grieve fully and completely so that I can move forward in hope. I especially ask for help with the secondary losses of __________

____

____

Amen.

Further Thoughts

DAY TWENTY-NINE

Taking Care of You

"Martha, Martha," the Lord answered, "you are worried and upset about many things, but only one thing is needed. Mary has chosen what is better, and it will not be taken away from her."

LUKE 10:41-42

Dr. Denise Fraser Vaselakos is passionate about helping women understand the protection that is theirs through Christ. As a psychologist and writer, she has spent many years working with women who are wounded, abandoned, and searching for a place of safety. One point she continually makes is that the Lord desires for women to care for themselves. When I asked her how this relates to living in hope, she told me:

> The world wants women to be busy all the time, but that leads to exhaustion. And exhausted women are not healthy women. An unhealthy, exhausted woman allows herself to be distracted, disrespected, and misused opening

> her up to worldly manipulation that leads to feelings of discouragement, anger, sadness, and hopelessness. Christ gives a woman permission to take care of herself, not in a selfish, self-serving worldly way, but in a self-caring way.

As Christian women, we're often told that godliness means overlooking our own needs. The more we serve, the more faith we must have. But Jesus said we are to love our neighbors as ourselves. That means our needs are equally important.

I personally struggle with this issue often. I tend to go a hundred miles an hour most of the time. It's easy for me to become exhausted physically, emotionally, and spiritually. I got away with this for a long time, but as I do my counseling internship, God has clearly been showing me that in order for me to pour into others, I need to be filled up first. This kind of self-care is not worldly indulgence; it's preparation for service. It's also a declaration that we are loved, valuable, worthy daughters of the King.

God made us complex beings with several different aspects to our lives. We have a body, soul, heart, mind, and spirit. Each part needs our care and attention. Sometimes we can get out of balance by focusing on one area and neglecting others. For example, we make time to nurture our spirit by reading the Bible but eat sugary foods all day that make us "crash and burn." Then we wonder why we don't feel joy. No one is in perfect sync, but by recognizing the importance of self-care in all of these areas, we can make choices that help us be strong, effective women.

Self-care is especially important when we're experiencing a difficult time in our lives. Our defenses are down, our energy is depleted, and we're more vulnerable. Dr. Vaselakos encourages women to consistently make the choice to care for themselves even when they don't feel like it or when others in their lives don't offer support. She points to women in the Bible, such as Abigail, Esther, and Ruth, who took steps to care for themselves and their families in difficult situations. She says, "Their lives did not take a course they might have predicted, but with God's guidance they were given permission by God to care for themselves and their families. And because these women were courageous enough to follow the Lord they loved, they lived lives of hopefulness and not despair."

Read

Luke 10:38-42

Reflect

What lies are you believing that are keeping you from taking care of yourself? What does God's Word say instead?

Which parts of your life are weak right now? Which are strong?

How can you take better care of yourself this week?

Respond

Lord, thank You for loving me and placing incredible value on each part of my life. I pray You will free me from whatever is keeping me from taking care of myself in the way You intended. I especially ask for help in overcoming the following obstacles:

Amen.

DAY THIRTY

Share Rather than Compare

Carry each other's burdens, and in this way you will fulfill the law of Christ.

GALATIANS 6:2

Carol Kent's life changed forever on October 25, 1999, when she received a phone call she never expected about her son, Jason. She learned that her beloved boy, now a grown man, had murdered his wife's ex-husband. Jason claimed he did so in order to protect his two stepdaughters from abuse. Regardless of his reasons, Jason was sentenced to life in prison without parole, and his parents began to adjust to a world that had been turned upside down.

In her book *A New Kind of Normal,* Carol shares her journey from shock, rage, and grief to hope, healing, and growth. She offers lessons from the tragedy that ripped her life apart like a tornado. In the epilogue she says, "Living in a new kind of normal has taught me that pain is pain is pain is pain. Repeatedly people come up to Gene and me after speaking engagements, and with urgency they say, 'I feel so guilty for feeling sorry for myself. Compared to the suffering you are experiencing, my pain is nothing.' Oh no, your pain is very real.... It's all pain."[28]

As a counseling intern, I often hear the same sentiment. Someone pours out a heart-wrenching story to me and then simply says, "But a lot of people have it worse than I do." That kind of comparison trivializes our hurt and keeps us from allowing ourselves to grieve. The worst pain you will ever feel is your own. That doesn't make you selfish or sinful; it just makes you human. Proverbs 14:10 says, "Each heart knows its own bitterness."

The raindrops that fall on us are the ones that soak our souls—even if we're only in a thunderstorm and someone we know is in a category 5 hurricane. We need to give ourselves permission to stop comparing our pain to that of others. It's okay to embrace that our hurt is real, legitimate, and worthy of our tears.

As we do, we'll be able to stop comparing and instead start sharing. Psychologist and writer Gary Oliver often says, "We only need to be broken once to know what it means to be broken."[29] In other words, we don't need to experience everything in order to have compassion. Even if we did go through the same thing as someone else, our journey would be different.

Instead we can say, "Your pain is not more or less significant than mine. What matters is that I know what it's like to hurt, and I will hurt with you." When we share rather than compare, we lighten the weight of grief both for those around us and for ourselves because we truly begin to carry each other's burdens.

Read

Galatians 6:2-10

Reflect

How do you compare yourself with others?

What would change if you began sharing rather than comparing?

Describe a time when you and another person shared your hurts with each other. How did that feel?

Respond

Lord, I'm so glad You look at us individually rather than comparing us to each other. Help me to do the same. I choose to own and acknowledge the following hurt rather than denying or diminishing it:

Amen.

DAY THIRTY-ONE

Look How Far You've Come

You are a chosen people, a royal priesthood, a holy nation, a people belonging to God, that you may declare the praises of Him who called you out of darkness into His wonderful light.

I PETER 2:9

For the past few weeks, you've been on a journey to hope. You've read, wrestled, and released. Perhaps you're even coming to the place where you want to share your journey with others who are hurting. Yet a part of you still wonders, *How can God use me?*

Ruth Graham, the daughter of Billy Graham, asked herself that question many times. Through her book *In Every Pew Sits a Broken Heart: Hope for the Hurting*, she shares about numerous struggles, including divorce, depression, and dealing with her husband's infidelity.

In the very first chapter, Ruth asserts,

> I am not qualified to write this book because I am Billy Graham's daughter. I am not qualified by

> position or vastness of expertise. I am qualified to write this book because I am flawed. Because I am a sinner saved by God's grace. Because I am headstrong and slow to learn. Because I have made mistakes. Many mistakes. And have failed often. My own story is not tidy. Nor is it simple. My story is messy and complicated and still being written.[30]

Her statements reminded me of another story, one told by Lamar Steiger, a community pastor for Fellowship Bible Church in Northwest Arkansas. Lamar struggled for many years with numerous issues and, at one point, even came close to taking his own life. Then God worked in a powerful way through the church and several men who came alongside Lamar to walk with him through his healing.

Several years later, when Lamar was asked to be a community pastor, he questioned, "How can you choose me in spite of all my struggles?" The response from Directional Leader Robert Cupp was clear. "We're not choosing you in spite of those things; we're choosing you because of them."

That answer reflects the grace God offers each of us. The apostle Paul could add his name to the list including Ruth Graham and Lamar Steiger. He also had a past that could have haunted him. He also faced many trials and great uffering in the present. Yet he realized he was called by God nd pursued that with all his heart.

Paul knew he could minister to sinners because he was ne. We look up to him, but at one point this spiritual giant ven said, "I was shown mercy so that in me, the worst of inners, Christ Jesus might display his unlimited patience as n example for those who would believe on Him and receive ternal life" (1 Timothy 1:16).

For you that statement might sound like, "I was shown race so that in me, a cancer survivor, Christ Jesus might lisplay his unlimited strength," or, "I was shown love so that n me, a grieving mother, Christ Jesus might display His nlimited hope." Whatever your story is, you have something o offer others.

It's said that you can only take someone as far as you have one yourself. Over the last few weeks, you have traveled a reat distance, perhaps even farther than you thought you ould go. Now it may be time for you to take the hand of omeone who is just starting their journey and say, "Come vith me. I've been this way before, and I know God will be vith us every step of the way."

Read

Peter 2:1-10

Reflect

What are some things God has shown you during the last few weeks that you can share with others?

Whom in your life can you encourage today?

What is a ministry God might have for you in the future because of this journey?

Respond

Lord, You waste nothing in our lives, including our hurts. I pray You will take the healing You have done in my life the last few weeks and show me how I can use it to help others. I especially pray for [*name person*]
and ask for an opportunity to be an encouragement in [*his/her*] life. Amen.

DAY THIRTY-TWO

Strength in Weakness

When I am weak, then I am strong.

2 Corinthians 12:10

Nick Vujicic entered the world without arms and legs. Facing countless challenges left Nick feeling depressed and even suicidal. However, he found strength in his faith and began to see how God seemed to use his disability in ways Nick hadn't expected. Now twenty-five years old, he is traveling the world sharing his message of achieving the impossible with God. Nick says, "If God can use a man without arms and legs to be His feet and hands, then He can use you." [31]

Nick has learned what many of us miss. In the places where we lack, God fills in the gaps. The apostle Paul expressed this when he described asking God three times to take away a challenge that he called "a thorn in my flesh."

We don't know exactly what that was, but we do know God's answer to Paul's request. God told him, "My grace is sufficient for you, for my power is made perfect in weakness." And Paul responded, "Therefore I will boast all the more gladly about my weaknesses, so that Christ's power may rest on me" (2 Corinthians 12:7-9).

It's easy to ask God to take away the hurts, difficulties, and weaknesses in our lives. It's far more challenging to ask, "Lord, how do you want to use this?" Yet, as Nick Vujicic discovered, that may be the turning point that takes us on an adventure of faith we never could have imagined. Nick has now visited more than nineteen countries, spoken to millions of people, and seen many give their lives to Christ. What seemed like loss has become a source of gain, both to Nick and the Kingdom of God. On his Web site, *Lifewithoutlimbs.org*, Nick says, "God took my life, one that others might disregard as having any significance and filled me with His purpose and showed me His plans to move hearts and lives toward Him. Understanding this, though faced with struggles, you can overcome too."

While we many not endure a physical disability, we will all have a "thorn in our flesh" that we may have a very hard time accepting or long for God to remove. Yet His loving answer may be as it was for Nick: *No, I will not take it away. But if you release it to Me, I will trade your weakness for My trength, your hurt for My hope, your defeat for My victory, your ain for My redemption.*

Read

2 Corinthians 12:1-10

Reflect

What is the "thorn in your flesh" right now?

How has God given you His strength through your weakness?

What are some areas where you still feel weak and need His help?

RESPOND

Lord, You know that I want You to remove this difficulty from my life. I've asked You to do so many times. But today I'm coming to ask You to show me how You want to use

---

---

in my life for Your purposes. I wouldn't have chosen this, but I do believe that You can make something good come from it Amen.

DAY THIRTY-THREE

The Divine Robinhood

You intended to harm me, but God intended it for good.
GENESIS 50:20

Heather Gemmen Wilson awoke one night to discover a rapist in her bedroom. Soon afterward she found that she was pregnant. In her book *Startling Beauty: My Journey from Rape to Restoration*, she describes how God brought healing to her life and gave her an amazing gift through her daughter.[32] In an article for *Today's Christian*, Heather says about Rachel, "She is a constant reminder to us, not of rape but of the startling beauty one can find hidden in tragedy."[33]

Did God plan for Heather to be raped? Of course not. Did He want her safety to be violated and her heart to be broken so He could show His goodness to the world? No. But is He committed to redeeming our entire lives and taking back what the enemy has stolen from us? Absolutely.

Jesus once told a parable about a master who went away and left his possessions in the hands of his servants to invest. When He returned, one servant made the statement, "You take out what you did not put in and reap what you did not sow" (Luke 19:21). This verse seems to portray God almost like a thief, but we know that the enemy is the one who has come "to steal and kill and destroy" (John 10:10).

As I pondered the blessings that seemed to grow in the broken places of my life, I came to understand what the servant meant in a different way. Where the enemy sows evil, God can still reap good. Like a divine Robinhood, God steals back what has been taken from us.

Joseph knew this well. When he was young, his brothers sold him into slavery. He endured a series of hardships, but over time God continued to promote him until Joseph became one of the most powerful leaders in Egypt. Eventually famine struck the land of Israel, and the brothers who betrayed him came looking for food. When Joseph revealed his identity to them, they feared what he would do. But Joseph showed them grace. Later in his life, he wisely told them, "You intended to harm me, but God intended it for good to accomplish what is now being done, the saving of many lives" (Genesis 50:20).

There is nothing beyond God's transforming power. No

storm is too destructive. No sin is too great. No seed sown is too toxic to be transformed into good. Heather Gemmen Wilson knows this each time she looks at her daughter. As Heather wrote in her blog, "Healing. Hope. Laughter. These are the things that define my life. Yes, I've experienced pain; but through it all, I have gained more than I have lost. I write so that when you see this is true for me, you can believe it will also be true for you."[34]

Read

Genesis 50:15-21

Reflect

What has the enemy tried to steal from you? ____________________

How is God restoring some of your losses? ____________________

What do you need God to give you right now? ____________________

____

____

____

____

Respond

Lord, thank You for being a God of restoration. The enemy may try to rob us, but You bring redemption. Today I need you to give me ____________________
in the midst of my loss. Amen.

DAY THIRTY-FOUR

The Center of the Storm

Shadrach, Meshach and Abednego came out of the fire, and the satraps, prefects, governors and royal advisers crowded around them. They saw that the fire had not harmed their bodies, nor was a hair of their heads singed; their robes were not scorched, and there was no smell of fire on them.

DANIEL 3:26-27

For the last few weeks, you've been taking some time in your day to be alone with God. You've committed to reading, reflecting, and responding to His heart. Our time together is coming to a close, and as it does, I encourage you to think about how you can continue spending intimate time with your heavenly Father. His presence is the eye of the storm, the place where you can find calm in the midst of all that's happening around you.

Shadrach, Meshach, and Abednego discovered this when they were thrown into a fiery furnace after refusing to bow down before the image of a pagan king. Even before being thrown into the furnace, they said, "The God we serve is able to save us from it, and he will rescue us from your hand, O king. But even if he does not, we want you to know, O king, that we will not serve your gods or worship the image of gold you have set up" (Daniel 3:17-18).

Their faith not only prepared them for this experience but also preserved them through it. When the king looked into the furnace, he said, "Look! I see four men walking around in the fire, unbound and unharmed, and the fourth looks like a son of the gods" (Daniel 3:25). Shadrach, Meshach, and Abednego emerged unharmed. They learned something important that day: God's presence makes all the difference. We can be in the midst of a fiery furnace and still be okay because He is there.

That's why it's so vital to set aside time each day to spend with God. While He's always with us and we're called to "pray without ceasing," there's something special about those moments when we pull away from everything else and have time alone with Him. His presence is a safe place for our hearts.

In *Resting Place: A Personal Guide to Spiritual Retreats*, Jane Rubietta encourages women to set aside a regular time to be restored and renewed by being in God's presence. She says, "Entering that rest—choosing God as our resting place—is more about our hearts and less about our hands. It's what's going on inside far more than what is going on outside. Rest is an internal state of soul, a relaxing into God's chest even when dashing through a day or season."[35]

When we take time to be with God—especially when things are difficult—we rediscover what Shadrach, Meshach, and Abednego did in the fiery furnace. It's not where we are in life but who is with us that truly makes all the difference.

Read

Daniel 3:12-30

Reflect

How has spending time with God the last few weeks made a difference in your life?

How can you continue spending time with Him when you're finished with this book?

What are some other ways you can make sure you stay close to God? ______

______

______

______

______

RESPOND

Lord, I want to live daily in Your presence. Help me to be disciplined and make spending time with You a priority. I especially ask for Your help in dealing with ______

______

______

which I find makes it harder for me to connect with You. Amen.

DAY THIRTY-FIVE

Finally Free

In my anguish I cried to the Lord,
and He answered by setting me free.
PSALM 118:5

One of my favorite movie scenes is in *Shawshank Redemption*.[36] Andy Dufresne is wrongly imprisoned for the murder of his wife. Over almost two decades, he carves a tunnel that eventually takes him to freedom. The final leg of his route requires him to crawl for 500 yards through a sewer pipe. Andy finally emerges from the filth and sludge into a pouring rain and raises his hands to the heavens in a clear declaration of freedom that's incredibly powerful and touching.

We've all known moments like the one Andy experienced. They're the times when, despite how much we had to go through, the length of time it took, or the rain that's falling around us, we know the journey was worth it and we'll never be the same.

Perhaps God brought you freedom in the last few weeks, when you were able to trust Him with your pain in a deeper way. Perhaps you decided to trade in a lie for the truth. Perhaps you finally chose hope even though your heart was still aching.

But imagine if, after that glorious moment in *Shawshank Redemption*, Andy had simply walked back to the front of the prison, knocked on the gate, and yelled, "Hey! Let me back in! I can check that off my to-do list now."

Of course we'd think that was crazy! However, we all do it sometimes. Breaking free is only the first step. *Staying* free is the difficult part. As Beth Moore says in her study *Breaking Free: Making Liberty in Christ a Reality in Life*, "When we get to heaven, we'll undoubtedly be 'Free at last!' Until then, we're challenged to make our newfound freedom last!"[37]

That's why I encourage you to pause and look back over how far you've come. Reread your answers to the questions. Look at what you've underlined. Ponder the prayers you've said along the way.

In which areas of your life have you been freed with God's help? And how will you make sure that you don't walk back into that prison after you've worked so hard to get out?

In *Shawshank Redemption*, Andy does just the opposite of the alternative I described. He heads for Mexico, to live his dream and embrace the freedom that took him so long to gain. We can do the same. That doesn't mean we won't hurt, have setbacks, or struggle again. It does mean that we choose to take what God has done in us and live it out. That requires courage, determination, and resilience. As the most compelling line in *Shawshank Redemption* says, “Fear can hold you prisoner. Hope can set you free.”

While we have to fight hard to get and stay free, God is the One who makes it possible. The key to moving forward in freedom is walking with Him, rain or shine, every step of the way.

Read

Psalm 118

Reflect

How has God brought you freedom in the last few weeks?

What are the areas in which you’d still like more freedom?

What steps will you take to ensure you continue to live in freedom and hope? ________

____

____

____

Respond

Lord, thank You for all You have done in my life and heart the last few weeks. I'm especially grateful for ________

____

____

I ask that You will help me to continue the changes You have begun in me. Teach me to live in freedom. Amen.

DAY THIRTY-SIX

Bruised Reeds and Smoldering Wicks

A bruised reed He will not break,
and a smoldering wick He will not snuff out.
MATTHEW 12:20

Brennan Manning, the best-selling author of books such as *The Ragamuffin Gospel*,[38] spoke recently at a local chapel service. I listened as this humble giant of the faith described how he almost lost everything after slipping into alcoholism. He recalls weaving down the street and stumbling to the ground as alcohol poisoning began to take hold of his body.

On all fours, with his face almost touching the dirty sidewalk of a busy city street, Brennan remembers hearing a still, small voice deep within his being. The Lord whispered, *Brennan, you are a bruised reed, and I will not crush you. You are a smoldering wick, and I will not snuff you out.* That kind of endless tenderness and scandalous grace drew Brennan back from the edge of destruction and became the message he has shared with millions.

What Christ spoke to Brennan, He says to each of us: *I will meet you in your weakness, and I will not press you down. Instead I will lift you up with love.*

During counseling sessions I often hear people say, "I was rejected by my parents. I was rejected by my spouse. But the worst wound of all has been my rejection by the church." If that is where you are today—if people have said things to you in God's name that have wounded you deeply, if you sit in the pew on Sunday morning and feel utterly alone in your pain, if you have been hurt by the very ones who were supposed to help you find healing—then please know that is not God's desire for you. We are imperfect people, and we are capable of tearing each other apart in ways that break our heavenly Father's heart.

Others may hurt you unintentionally, but we do have an enemy that's openly trying to destroy us. The devil is described as a lion looking for someone to devour (1 Peter 5:8). Lions look for the weakest member of the herd, isolate that animal, and then move in for the kill. They are experts at taking advantage of those who are vulnerable.

We can sometimes attribute to God what's actually the work of the enemy in our lives. But our Lord is not like a prowling lion but rather like a protective shepherd. When a member of a shepherd's flock is hurt, the shepherd rescues that animal, tends to its wounds, keeps it close by his side to protect it from further harm, and even carries it on his shoulders. A shepherd sees weakness as an opportunity for loving care.

As Brennan Manning discovered that day, God often shows His love most when we deserve it least. Others may try to take advantage of our weakness or leave us alone in our pain, but our Shepherd never will. Close your eyes for a moment and hear Him speak to your wounded heart: *My child, you are a bruised reed, and I will not crush you. You are a smoldering wick, and I will not snuff you out.*

Read

Matthew 12:9-21

Reflect

Is it difficult for you to experience God's love when you feel weak or wounded? Why or why not?

In what ways do you think the enemy could be trying to attack you during this time in your life? ______

______

______

______

______

How do you need God to be your loving and protective Shepherd today? ______

______

______

______

______

Respond

Lord, I feel especially vulnerable during this time of my life. I specifically ask for You to protect me from ______

______

I also ask for You to strengthen me and gently lift me up with love. Amen.

DAY THIRTY-SEVEN

The Last Tear

Record my lament;
list my tears on your scroll—
are they not in your record?
PSALM 56:8

When her sister Tara was killed in an accident during her senior year of high school, Heidi Fraanz had to say good-bye far too soon. While Heidi has made it through the worst of the storm and is even leading a group to help others with their losses, she still grieves at times. On what would have been her sister's twenty-seventh birthday, Heidi forwarded to me a devotional from *Daily Bread*, written by Dave Branon.

Branon appropriately began with these words, "When I asked a friend how she was doing four years after the sudden death of her husband, she said, 'I feel I am healing. Tears tend to burn my eyes rather than pour down my face. To me, that is a measure of healing.'" Branon had lost his own teenage daughter, and reflecting on this, he talks about how grief is a process that takes a lifetime. He insightfully says, "Indeed, God has promised that He will wipe away all tears in heaven (Revelation 7:17), but until then the healing will be incomplete." [39]

When I work with hurting people, they often ask, "When will the pain stop?" We all want to write a big "The End" on the last page of our story and move on with our lives. But the uncomfortable answer to that question is, grief takes longer than most of us expect. For a major loss, like a death or divorce, one to five years is a fairly common amount of time.

Even after that amount of time, your grief will not be totally gone. If you've been wondering, "Why can't I get over this?" then breathe a sigh of relief. The frequency and intensity of your bouts of sorrow will steadily decrease. You will gradually have more joy than sadness in your life again. But you may still hear a song, see a face, or look at the date on a calendar and find your grief returning for an unexpected visit.

God truly is the only one who can wipe every tear from our eyes, and one day He will. As Heidi has learned, the story of our loss can only be completed in eternity. While we may not understand it, God is still writing each word with love. He promises to give us strength, peace, and hope for each page. His Son died for us so that our sorrows could be healed and we could be in a place without pain forever. Christ's final words on the cross were "It is finished." And on the day He wipes away the last tear from our eyes, those will be the closing words in the story of our heartaches as well.

Read

Psalm 56

Reflect

Does the amount of time it takes to grieve a loss surprise you? Why or why not?

What do you most need God to give you for your journey right now (for example: strength, peace, joy)?

Close your eyes and imagine the Lord wiping away your last tear. How does your heart feel when you think of that day?

Respond

Lord, I know that one day You will wipe away every tear from my eyes. Until that time, I need Your help to make it through this journey. Today I just want to say to You

Amen.

DAY THIRTY-EIGHT

Your Companion for the Journey

He will give you another Counselor to be with you forever—the Spirit of truth...
You know Him, for He lives with you and will be in you.
JOHN 14:16-17

Dick and Rick Hoyt have competed in dozens of marathons and numerous triathlons as a father-son team. What makes this pair so unusual is that Rick has severe cerebral palsy and can't walk or talk. He has learned to communicate using a special computer. Doctors encouraged the Hoyts to place their son in a home. However, Dick and his wife were determined to raise him like any other child.

At age fifteen Rick asked his father to push him in a wheelchair so he could be part of a race raising money for charity. Although they finished second to last, the race felt like a triumph. Rick told his father he "didn't feel handicapped" when they were competing. Twenty-five years and over eighty marathons and eight triathlons later, Team

Hoyt is still going strong. For Dick, now over sixty-five, this process hasn't been easy. The competitions are physically challenging, as well as mentally and emotionally draining. Nevertheless, for Dick every minute of exertion and every mile of endurance is worth it.

Imagine if we each had someone like him who would run the race of life with us—someone who would do for us what we could never do for ourselves, who would see our inherent value and love us just as we are, who would take us all the way to the finish line. Jesus told us that we do have someone just like that in our lives and hearts. Before He went to the cross, He told His disciples, "I will ask the Father, and He will give you another Counselor to be with you forever—the Spirit of truth. The world cannot accept Him, because it neither sees Him nor knows Him. But you know Him, for He lives with you and will be in you" (John 14:16-17).

For many of us, the Holy Spirit is the most mysterious member of the Trinity. But understanding His role is vital to living fully, especially during difficult times. The Holy Spirit comforts, empowers, and leads us. He speaks truth to our hearts when we need it most. Like Dick Hoyt with his son, the Holy Spirit does in and through us what we could never do for ourselves.

If Rick looked for his father during a race, he probably wouldn't be able to see him. That's because Dick is always behind his son, exerting all of his energy to move him forward. But Rick can feel the wheels of his chair turning, he can hear the encouraging words being spoken to him, he can see the finish line drawing closer and closer. In much the same way, we can trust that the Holy Spirit is always with us. As we rely completely on Him, He'll work on our behalf, guide us with love, and ensure we're triumphant no matter what we may face.

Read

John 14:15-31

Reflect

Describe the Holy Spirit and His role in your life.

How has the Holy Spirit helped you during this time?

What are some ways you could find out more about who the Holy Spirit is and what He does? ______

______

______

______

Respond

Holy Spirit, I'm so glad You're always with me. Thank You for being my comforter, counselor, encourager, and guide. I'm especially grateful for the way You've ______

______

______

Help me know and understand You better. Amen.

DAY THIRTY-NINE

The "Do What You Can" Plan

I can do everything through Him who gives me strength.
PHILIPPIANS 4:13

I remember driving along one day and thinking, "When things get back to normal, I'll start exercising." Then I thought about how I'd work out every day, eat right, and be the healthiest person around. Suddenly I realized I'd been having the same conversation with myself for years and nothing had changed. My unrealistic expectations were keeping me from making any progress.

I decided to create the "Do What You Can" plan. That meant that if I had time for ten sit-ups, that's what I'd do. If I had time for five minutes of walking, that was great. Over the last two and a half years, the "Do What You Can" plan has helped me reach my goals. If I'd stuck with my original expectations, I'd still be driving around saying, "When things get back to normal...."

I hope this book has offered moments of connection with God, helpful ideas, and new insights to apply in your life. The temptation, of course, is to look at those opportunities and say, "When things get back to normal, then I'll...." Things are never going to get back to normal, though—not the old normal. Loss and difficulties alter our lives in ways that can't be undone. Yes, we can move forward, but it's in a new and different direction. Ecclesiastes 11:4 says, "Whoever watches the wind will not plant; whoever looks at the clouds will not reap." In other words, if we're waiting for "the right time," then we may be waiting forever.

We also sometimes expect so much of ourselves that we end up feeling defeated and don't try at all. Philippians 4:13 says, "I can do everything through Him who gives me strength." But it doesn't say, "I have to do it all right now." Give yourself permission to go slow, take one step at a time, and pat yourself on the back for every bit of progress. It's okay just to do what you can each day.

That's especially true if you're in the middle of a storm and just trying to survive. If all you have the energy for is whispering a one-sentence prayer to God, then go for it. If it takes everything within you just to have coffee with a friend, then that's success. If you make it through an hour without feeling grumpy, then celebrate. We often require far more of ourselves than God requires of us. There's a sentence at the top of my journal that says, "God values growth and connection more than perfection."

When I started exercising, I began using weights a lot of the time. I learned that each time you lift a weight, you actually create a tear in the muscle. When your body repairs that tear, it makes you stronger. Over time your endurance increases and you can lift more weight.

God has made us emotionally in much the same way. Our hearts can only handle so much at a time, but if we continue to partner with God to do what we can each day, we'll discover those little gains add up to a big difference in our lives.

Read

Philippians 4:6-13

Reflect

What has been holding you back from just doing what you can?

What unrealistic expectations do you have for yourself right now? How can you give yourself grace?

What are some small, realistic steps God is asking you to take?

Respond

Lord, thank You for giving me far more grace than I often give myself. I pray that You'll help me see clearly what You're asking me to do and what I'm just placing on myself. Today I release the following unrealistic expectations to You:

and instead commit to

Amen.

DAY FORTY

Beyond the Rain

When the dove returned to him in the evening, there in its beak was a freshly plucked olive leaf! Then Noah knew that the water had receded from the earth.

GENESIS 8:11

For forty days and nights, rain fell and covered the earth with floodwaters, extinguishing all visible life outside the ark. Noah and his family waited for hope to reappear. Finally the storm subsided, the waters receded, and life began again. Noah's first sign of this renewal of life came from a dove released from the ark who returned with an olive leaf in its beak.

For forty days and nights, we've walked through a storm together. While the rain may still be falling, I pray that hope has begun to appear in your life again. I also pray that what you've read in these pages will make the other storms in your life easier to endure. And those other storms will come. As long as we live in this broken, fallen world, there will be days when the skies grow dark.

That's why my heart's desire is that you've come to believe in a deeper way that, while God may not cause the rain in our lives, He's committed to redeeming every drop. He wants to use it to quench our thirsty souls, bring forth life from the barren desert of our hearts, and grow a garden of blessings filled with a beauty we never imagined possible in the midst of our pain. Rain is inevitable; hope and resilience are optional. But I truly believe with God's help, both can be ours no matter what we may face.

I'm so grateful you let me share this journey with you. I offer my continued prayers and these final words as gifts to you, dear daughter of God:

You are a woman of strength—
more than a conqueror,
able to do all things,
a warrior and princess
in the Kingdom of God.
The Lord has given you
all you need
and made you
all you need to be
for victory.
So go forth, strong sister,
with an umbrella of love,

a heart full of grace,
and a determination
to never stop
until God redeems
each raindrop in your life
and you receive every
olive leaf of hope
our heavenly Father has for you.

Read

Genesis 9:8-17

Reflect

What has God spoken to your heart in the last forty days?

How can you continue to seek hope in your life?

What will you always remember from this journey? ______

______

______

______

______

Respond

Lord, I'm so thankful for everything You've shown me during the last forty days. I will always remember ______

______

______

______

______

Please continue to use the storms in my life to bring new growth, healing, and hope to my heart. Amen.

Further Thoughts

Endnotes

1. Eldredge, John and Stasi, *Captivating: Unveiling the Mystery of a Woman's Soul* (Nashville: Thomas Nelson, Inc., 2005).

2. *Forrest Gump* (Paramount, 2001).

3. Lewis, C.S., *The Lion, the Witch and the Wardrobe* (New York: HarperCollins Publishers, 1994), p.86.

4. Ortberg, John, *If You Want to Walk on Water, You've Got to Get Out of the Boat* (Grand Rapids: Zondervan, 2001), p. 17.

5. Ortberg, p. 17.

6. Oliver, Carrie, *Updates on Carrie Oliver* (www.carrieshealth.com), June 20, 2005 (http://www.carrieshealth.com/JournalEntries/2005/06-20-05.html).

7. Personal communication from Jamie Zumwalt, Fellowship Bible Church, Rogers, Arkansas, August 16, 2008.

8. Alcorn, Randy, *Heaven* (Wheaton, Ill.: Tyndale House Publishers, Inc., 2004), p. 460.

9. Alcorn, p. 417.

10. Cowman, Mrs. Charles, *Streams in the Desert* (public domain, retrieved from http://www.crosswalk.com/devotionals/desert/).

11. Lewis, C.S., *A Grief Observed* (San Francisco: HarperCollins Publishers, 1996), p.69

12. Smith, Angie, *Bring the Rain* (http://audreycaroline.blogspot.com/).

13. Cloud, Henry, PhD, and Townsend, John, PhD, Boundaries: *When to Say Yes, When to Say No to Take Control of Your Life* (Grand Rapids, Mich.: Zondervan, 1992), p. 32

14. Cowman.

15. Personal communication from Julie Sawyer Phillips.

16. "Praise You in this Storm," Casting Crowns, *Lifesong* (Reunion, 2005).

17. Hall, Mark, Lifestories: *Finding God's "Voice of Truth" Through Everyday Life* (Provident-Integrity Distribution, 2006), excerpted at http://www.christianitytoday.com/music/commentaries/hegivesandtakesaway.html.

18. Hall, "He Gives and Takes Away," (Christianmusictoday.com, August 2006, retrieved from http://www.christianitytoday.com/music/commentaries/hegivesandtakesaway.html).

19. Miller, Terry, "Inspiring Baby Stories You Shared with Us," DaySpring.com, retrieved from http://store.dayspring-store.com/babystories2.html.

20. *Cast Away* (20th Century Fox, 2002).

21. Arrington, Candy, "Don't Forget to Live," *Today's Christian*, November/December 2004, Vol. 42, No. 4, p. 56

22. McDonald, Gordon, *Ordering Your Private World* (Nashville: Thomas Nelson, Inc., 2003), p.12.

23. Wright, H. Norman, Resilience: *Rebounding When Life's Upsets Knock You Down* (Ann Arbor, Mich.: Vine Books), p.17.

24. Rohn, Jim. Speaker and writer, quoted in online database.

25. Guthrie, Nancy, *Holding onto Hope: A Pathway through Suffering to the Heart of God* (Carol Stream, Ill.: Tyndale House Publishers, 2004), p.86.

26. Wright, H. Norman, *Recovering from Losses in Life* (Grand Rapids: Revell, div. of Baker Publishing Group, 2006), pp.21-22.

27. Wright, p.21.

28. Kent, Carol, *A New Kind of Normal* (Nashville: Thomas Nelson, Inc., 2007), p.219.

29. Oliver, Gary, *Christian Foundations* (John Brown University, Siloam Springs, Ark., graduate counseling program class, 2007).

30. Graham, Ruth, *In Every Pew Sits a Broken Heart: Hope for the Hurting* (Grand Rapids: Zondervan, 2004), p.13.

31. Vujicic, Nick, "TBN Highlights for 2007," aired December 31, 2007.

32. Gemmen, Heather, *Startling Beauty: My Journey from Rape to Restoration* (Colorado Springs: Cook Communications, 2004).

33. Gemmen, "Loving the Rapist's Child," *Today's Christian*, March/April 2005, Vol. 43, No. 2, p.22.

34. Wilson, Heather Gemmen, http://www.heathergemmenblog.blogspot.com/.

35. Rubietta, Jane, *Resting Place: A Personal Guide to Spiritual Retreats* (Downers Grove, Ill.: InterVarsity Press, 2005), p.22.

36. *Shawshank Redemption* (Castle Rock, 2007).

37. Moore, Beth, *Breaking Free: Making Liberty in Christ a Reality in Life* (Nashville: LifeWay Press, 2004), p.218.

38. Multnomah Publishing, 1990, 2005.

39. Branon, Dave, "A Measure of Healing," *Our Daily Bread*, September 13, 2008, retrieved from http://www.rbc.org/devotionals/our-daily-bread/2008/09/13/devotion.aspx.